Foreword by Charlie "Tremendous" Jones

A Fortune to Share

— it's yours, if you want it!

Paul J. Meyer
New York Times Best-Selling Author

A Fortune to Share

Published by
Executive Books
206 West Allen Street
Mechanicsburg, PA 17055
717-766-9499   800-233-2665
Fax: 717-766-6565
www.ExecutiveBooks.com

Paperback ISBN: 978-1-933715-74-2

Book Production Services Provided by Gregory A. Dixon

Printed in the United States of America

Table of Contents

Foreword

I'm humbled and honored to write the foreword to one of the most inspiring books I've ever read by one of the most inspiring men I've ever known. There are many Tremendous ways to describe Paul J. Meyer, but what makes him unique is that his humility matches his fortune.

This book is for all of us, because we all hunger to be more, to have more, and to impact more. Paul J. Meyer has made it his life's work to help people reach their full potential. That means a lot, but what speaks even louder are the millions of voices that have been positively impacted by this man.

Beginning at an early age, Paul began uncovering the gifts of life that we all are entitled to. He has come to see that we can lay claim to virtually anything we wish. *"As a man thinketh in his heart, so is he,"* says an ancient writer.

Inside this book, you will find truths that will challenge you to reach higher than ever before. You will be motivated. You will be encouraged. You will be given a lot. And you will see that you too have a fortune to share.

In 1960, after an impressively successful insurance career, Paul took what he learned as a master salesman, manager, leader, and motivator of others and began a corporation dedicated to "motivating people to their full potential."® That flagship company has grown into numerous organizations worldwide that have almost three billion dollars in combined sales.

Other areas of interest have also developed into businesses owned by Meyer and his family, including publishing, education, printing, finance, legal insurance, auto racing, nutrition products, aviation, manufacturing, real estate, and much more. His entrepreneurial expertise has propelled him and his family to investments in numerous companies and ownership of more than forty corporations throughout the world.

As Paul's friend for more than fifty years, I have observed that the greatest contributing factor to his long-standing success is his attitude. He is telling it like it is in this book.

4

His tremendous attitude, combined with his success habits and infinite thirst for knowledge, sets him apart from the typical businessperson. These traits have not only sustained him through the dramatic ups and downs frequently characterizing the risks and rewards of business ownership, but they have also catapulted him to phenomenal success.

Paul J. Meyer's philosophy and attitudes have literally helped millions of people reach more of their full potential. The rewards earned by his achievements have been used by Meyer to help even more people.

He accepts the abundance — and responsibilities — with the attitude of a steward. He views the riches of life as a trust and himself as the trustee. The beneficiaries of his inheritance are those who have used his writings to find purpose and success in their own lives, and those who have been helped by one of the many foundations he and his family have established.

As you read, you will see how Paul's conscious choice to feed his mind diligently and carefully with only the richest, most positive ideas available has created his indomitable attitude ... and his incredible fortune. And what he has gained, he generously shares with you.

Inside this treasure book are valuable seeds of success. Plant these seeds in your own mind and soul and you will reap the happiness and success your Creator has set aside for you when you seek it and work for it.

It's yours if you want it.

Charlie "Tremendous" Jones

5

"Your inheritance depends on you ... only you can turn your dreams into reality."

— Paul J. Meyer

Chapter #1
A World of Abundance

— *Yours for the taking*

When my brother, sister, and I were growing up, we were dirt poor.

We just didn't know it.

We lived in the garage for 10 years while our dad fixed up and built the rest of the house.

That's just the way it was.

And when I told my parents I wanted a bike more than anything else, guess where my dad took me?

He took me to the junkyard!

We scrounged around for an old discarded bike that could be re-built. I found an old, bent rusty bicycle that we hauled home and took apart, piece-by-piece. We then straightened, cleaned, greased, and painted until it was ready.

At first glance, it seemed I got ripped of, a raw deal, short-changed, the short end of the stick:

> **"I have learned that the whole world is mine for the taking ... and that if I assume that I will get nothing, I will indeed get nothing."**
> — Paul J. Meyer

- Did I have the nicest bike on the block?

  <u>NO!</u>

- Did I have the newest bike on the block?

  <u>NO!</u>

- Did I have the money for a bike?

  <u>NO!</u>

- Did I have a rich relative to buy me a bike?

  <u>NO!</u>

But don't feel sorry for me. I genuinely believe that I came out ahead in the end.

Let me explain:

- Did I spend time with my Dad fixing that bike?

  <u>Yes</u>, and it was some of the best fun I had with him!

- Did I learn how to fix my own bike?

  <u>Yes</u>, and I went on to buy old bicycles, fix them up, and resell them. I sold over 300 refurbished bicycles as a teenager, and made good money doing it!

"Adversity reveals genius, prosperity conceals it."

— Horace

- **Did I gain from the experience?**

  <u>You bet!</u> I learned how to take responsibility for myself. That reality has served me well!

- **Did I come out ahead?**

  <u>Absolutely!</u> In fact, learning how to be resourceful and think outside of the box has positively impacted my life in countless ways!

And when we had rebuilt a few bikes, my dad laughed and said, "Let's do the same thing with a car." And we did!

I learned so many valuable lessons, and these early experiences laid the foundation for my lifelong, invincible attitude of finding a way — or making one!

The world is mine!

As a youngster, I rode my bike seven miles into town — San Jose, California — to buy some powdered milk, day-old bread, and a few other items my mother needed. When we had the money, we would buy fresh milk and fresh bread at a grocery store not far from our home.

On one particular trip to San Jose, my mother told me that if I had any money left I could buy a watermelon. There was just enough left over!

I loaded my purchases into my bike basket that day and headed home. I remember that bike ride like it was yesterday:

> **"A mind stretched by a new idea, never regains its original dimensions."**
> — Oliver Wendell Holmes

A FORTUNE TO SHARE

the sun was shining,
the wind was just right,
the blue sky sparkled above me,
spring flowers were everywhere,
and the birds were singing.

The world was my cornucopia!

I felt happy from the top of my head to the tips of my toes. I reveled in my abundance. I had inherited the riches of the entire creation!

Did I really own it all?

Of course not, but my attitude of positive expectancy was taking root in my young heart.

Years earlier, I had asked my mother, **"Who owns all the birds, the flowers, and the trees?"**

"You own them if you are wise enough to enjoy them," she answered.

I said, **"How about the stars in the sky?"**

She said, **"You own the stars, too, if you choose to."**

So I said to myself, **"I'll just own them. Then I'll have something to share with others that will never be used up."**

The seed of belief had been planted in me that the riches of all creation belonged to me if I wanted them and claimed them.

> **"Unless you try to do something beyond what you have already mastered, you will never grow."**
> — Ralph Waldo Emerson

And I wanted and claimed them!

My abundance exceeds money, houses, and lands, and we aren't even talking about money.

It's yours, if you want it!

Since my childhood I have nourished that seed of truth, and it has flourished. I hold the power to claim a magnificent inheritance:

It all depends on me — the way I choose to look at life,
the way I think, and
the way I act.

There are signs everywhere that say, **Posted. Keep Out!** or **Private-No Trespassing**.

But I never notice them! Nothing restricts my enjoyment of the beauty of creation. That beauty belongs to anyone who appreciates it and claims it!

I have learned that the whole world is mine for the taking, and that if I assume that I will get nothing, then I will indeed get nothing.

Approaching life with such a negative attitude
would cause me to fall into despair
and oblivion, and
finally, to die.

Since you get from life exactly what you expect, why not choose to dream marvelous, magnificent dreams!

"Make your life be the song never forgotten, the painting whose colors leap off the canvas, and the greatest story ever told."
— Gina Chong-You

Then work to transform those dreams into reality.

None of us should have any trouble accepting life's abundance. *I have always wondered why anyone would ever doubt the abundance of human potential.* All people have talents, abilities, and qualities they never dreamed existed.

Early in life I realized that vast fortunes exist in every person. All we have to do to inherit them is to claim them and to use them.

You have it within you!

Here are some of the keys to believing in the abundance of the universe and the bountiful fortune we can all share:

My life is like an orchestra. I have been given the baton by my Creator. I have inherited notes that I can use in any combination I choose.

Great masters, like —

- Mozart,
- Chopin,
- Beethoven, and
- Tchaikovsky

— all used the same basic notes that I have in my possession to compose beautiful music. I can make any kind of music I want!

And so can you.

"The future belongs to those who believe in the beauty of their dreams."
— Eleanor Roosevelt

My life is like a painting. I have inherited all the colors of the rainbow and I can choose any size brush or any design. I can mix ten gallons of paint or one million gallons of paint to create a panoramic canvas.

My inheritance came with no restrictions or limitations. I can use one color and one size brush and paint one boring picture ... or I can paint like Da Vinci or Rembrandt.

The choice is mine!

My life is like the great literature of the world. I inherited twenty-six letters in the English alphabet. If I had been born in a different country with a different language, a different set would have been given to me to use for writing and speaking.

The basic set of letters or characters is all that every legendary author has ever used to give us great literature.

I have the exact same tools in my possession, as do you.

Enough to share

Decades ago when I started selling for the world's largest exclusive weekly premium life insurance company, I lived in a modest house trailer. Even though I had already improved my lot in life considerably, I wanted greater things.

All of the trailers were parked north and south. *I wanted to be*

> **"Man should not consider his material possessions his own, but as common to all, so as to share them without hesitation when others are in need."**
> — Thomas Aquinas

unique! I persuaded the owner of the trailer park to allow me to use two spaces and to turn my trailer east and west.

Then I built a little picket fence around my trailer. I had a sign painted and hung out in front of my house.

The sign read:
"Meyer's Mansion."

I still lived in a trailer park, but that sign was to me a tangible, positive affirmation that:

1. **I had inherited a fortune** and

2. **I should encourage others to share in this marvelous inheritance.**

My fortune is far more valuable than any amount of money or material things. I have gone literally from rags to riches, but the most precious treasure I own is the satisfaction I receive from encouraging others to share in this fortune.

Time and experience have reinforced and expanded my desire to share my fortune with others.

I do not *give* to *get*.

I give because I have a need to *give*.

I need to *share*.

I believe rich rewards come to those who share the fortune they have inherited. What has happened to me was predicted centuries

---

"Lord, grant that I may always desire more than I accomplish."

— Michelangelo

---

ago in the Bible (Luke 6:38) where it says:

> *Give, and gifts will be given to you; a good measure,*
> *pressed down, shaken together, and running over will be*
> *put into your hands. For with the same measure that you*
> *use, it will be measured back to you.*

A lot of people have a big goal that they charge toward, and this is good. The problem is that most of these people who do indeed reach their big goal will, in time, begin to feel lost. Goal accomplished. They will have "arrived."

But they will have a looming question over their heads, "What next?"

When you realize that you have a fortune to share,
you never "arrive."

You never settle in and quit
charging forward.

Instead, you keep on going. You dream new dreams.

And you share.

Nobody ever "arrives." In reality, they are stopping beside the road of life. Don't let this happen to you. Choose to keep going. Choose to be a giver. Choose to share.

You have plenty to spare!

"I wake up every morning without giving mental recognition to the possibility of defeat."

— Paul J. Meyer

"By rejecting all negative thoughts and filling your mind with powerful positive thoughts, you are setting the law of attraction in motion to your benefit!"

— Paul J. Meyer

Chapter #2
You Attract What You Think

— Just like a magnet!

A magnet reveals the simple law of attraction like nothing else can. If you place a magnet close to a piece of metal, bam! The two objects slam together!

You have to work pretty hard to keep them apart. That is because, quite obviously, the magnet is attracting the piece of metal.

This truth also applies to attitudes, and here is how it works:

A positive attitude attracts positive results.

The power of a positive attitude is far-reaching.

It is unstoppable.

It will not be denied.

And it goes well beyond the boundaries of our thought processes.

In contrast, when people have negative attitudes, they attract negative results. **They get exactly what they expect:**

- **Negative consequences**

- **No return on their investment.**

"The destiny of man is in his own soul."
— Herodotus

- More disappointment.

- More of the same old.

When people allow fear, worry, doubt, indecision, and other forms of negative thinking to determine their mental attitude, they effectively shut off their positive attitudes.

They can only attract negatives ... because the only magnet they are using is a negative one!

When they focus on the *"cannots"* rather than the *"cans,"* the outcome is predictably negative.

Hard work does NOT necessarily bring success

A lot of people appear to be working feverishly, always busy, but they never reach the goals they desire. No matter how hard they work, they can never attract a successful and positive situation in life.

Why? Because they are working on the wrong things!

Look at it this way.

If you know there are 10 specific steps to take to reach your goal, **wouldn't you agree that doing anything other than those specific 10 steps is a waste of time?**

If people are not taking steps toward their goals, no amount of work, even good intentioned, will ever result in achieving the goals.

"Accept the challenges so that you may feel the exhilaration of victory."
— General George S. Patton

The principle, "Work hard and you'll succeed," is true to a point, but it is not the whole truth. You must work hard AND smart. That is why, in order to be successful, all efforts must:

be lined up,

consistent with, and

in support of achieving the desired goals.

In short, think your goals through, plan them out, and then work hard to achieve them. Working hard on the wrong thing will do you no good! When you work hard at working smart, that is when you get the high payoff!

Believe in the law of attraction

For the law of attraction to work most powerfully in our lives, we must *believe in it*. With a magnet, you must first *believe* that the magnet possesses power.

Attracting the nails has to be *mentally* accomplished before it can be *physically* accomplished.

It isn't that your mental "power" enables the magnet to work. **Not at all!** Instead, you must believe the magnet will attract, or you wouldn't even try it.

True? You must believe before you will try.

You have confidence that the magnet will attract, but until you actually put the magnet close to the metal object you want to attract,

---

"Human beings can alter their lives by altering the attitudes of their mind."
— William James

---

nothing is going to happen.

When you set goals, you must *believe* that you can reach those goals and then take action on that belief. **I never give recognition to the possibility of defeat in any area of my life.**

My belief, my faith, my attitude, my attention, and my actions are like a giant magnet, attracting the results I wish to attract.

**No science, dogma, creed, or religion in the world
will let me attract anything if I have
a negative mental attitude and
a disbelief that it will ever happen.**

Or to say it another way:

*If you are negative, you won't attract anything positive
into your life.*

Belief in the law of attraction has to be …

in our bone marrow,

in our white corpuscles and red corpuscles,

in our muscles, and

in our skin.

It must show …

in our eyes,

"Chance favors the prepared mind."
— Louis Pasteur

20

be reflected in our voices,

show in our walk, and

be felt from the energy we generate.

I live with belief in this principle.

Nobody will ever say about me, "He lacks confidence" or "He has no faith in what he is doing" or "He doesn't really think he can attract the positive results he is seeking."

Not a chance!

I am a magnet and the law of attraction is alive and well in me!

Since magnets attract ... put them to use!

A magnet sitting on a shelf, not doing what it was designed to do, is much like a complacent person whose attitude and actions declare, "I fear taking action. I am afraid of taking a chance."

In reality, people like this fear reaching out for more.

Why? *Because they do not believe they can get more.*

Their disbelief and complacency reveals their thinking — *that they have found some type of "security" in assuming a do-nothing position.* They build a wall around their limited self-image to protect it and they live out their days in negative expectancy.

Not for me!

"Knock the 't' off of can't."
— Coleman Cox

And not for you!

Just as a magnet is not designed to sit on a shelf doing nothing, you were also not created for a stark, immobile, lackluster, unfulfilling existence either.

Magnets have power. You have power. Put that power to use!

Consider this profound principle:

> **People are happy and fulfilled only when they use their lives to fulfill the noble and inspiring purposes for which their Creator designed them.**

Unless you use the power within you, you will forever feel unfulfilled. But when you use that power … *the world had better watch out!*

How the mind works

No magnet attracts and repels the same object. It doesn't work that way. It's either positive or negative.

Similarly, **faith and fear cannot coexist in the same mind**. Your mind is limited to either up or down, forward or backward, on or off.

There is no middle ground.

Consider this sad truth:

People who are full of fear, worry, doubt, indecision, and

"Ambition is the shadow of a dream."
— William Shakespeare

---

other negative thinking _cannot_ at the same time possess faith, confidence, belief, and positive expectancy.

It's totally impossible!

They want something they cannot have.

They want something they will not have!

It's the law and it cannot be broken.

And that's all there is to it.

The only way to change this law from working against you ... _is to make it work for you!_ The law continues, always and forever.

Attract what you want

Here is the law of attraction:

You attract to yourself exactly what your thoughts attract.

Typically, we hear the negative version, which states:

You cannot attract to your self what your thought repels.

But the law of attraction is one of the most positive success principles that we can apply to our lives on a daily basis.

> **"You will become as small as your controlling desire, as great as your dominant aspiration."**
> — James Allen

A FORTUNE TO SHARE

It's wonderful!

And it works constantly.

All the time!

There's no stopping it!

If you persistently and constantly entertain thoughts of belief and positive expectancy, your body responds positively because of the constructive actions taken on the basis of positive attitudes.

But not everyone sees life from that perspective. For whatever the reason, they:

- **possess a poverty mentality,**

- **don't think they can do it,**

- **don't think they can handle success,**

- **are convinced that only a limited supply of success exists and that there is not enough to go around to everyone who wants some of it, or**

- **come up with another excuse.**

I wish they — like me — had a no-limitations belief in themselves, in their Creator, in the potential of other people, and in the abundance of the world!

> **"Make no little plans: they have no magic to stir men's blood and probably themselves will not be realized."**
> — Daniel H. Burnham

I used to say, **"I'm going out to shake the money tree today,"** and I meant it!

The roads are lined with gold, with sales, with friends, or with anything you might need!

The trees are bending down to the ground with the answers you need.

The vines are breaking with the supplies you seek.

The fields are overflowing with the resources you want.

It is simply a matter of attitude.

Decide what you want!

Coachella Valley, in the Southern California desert, is one of the most beautiful small valleys I have ever seen anywhere.

If you have been there, you know what I'm talking about! It is about 30 miles long and 10 miles wide. It was not made by forces of nature, but by the hard work of human hands.

Years ago who would ever have thought this oasis was possible in the midst of a sandy desert? *Certainly not an individual with a negative mentality!*

Someone with an abundance attitude and a positive expectancy saw the possibilities in the middle of this desert and developed a

> **"We're about as happy as we make up our minds to be."**
> — Abraham Lincoln

beautiful oasis.

Consider these truths:

If you want plenty, you have to think plenty.

If you want wealth, you have to think wealth.

If you want success, you have to think success.

If you want health, you have to think health.

And if you want happiness, you must think happiness.

Abraham Lincoln said, "We're about as happy as we make up our minds to be."

That is such an incredible and accurate statement. It is a choice. And the good news is that we can choose.

Attracting the conditions you wish to attract,
like a magnet,
is essential for
bringing those conditions
into reality.

People often call me lucky, as if my achievements — wealth, success, health, and happiness — just happened by accident. **But nothing in my life is the result of luck.**

My achievements are the results of faith, perseverance, preparation,

---

"If you assume you will get nothing,
you will get nothing ... but the reverse
also holds true!"

— Paul J. Meyer

---

and the unstoppable law of attraction.

Now, when people call you lucky, you'll know what to say!

> **"'Impossible' is a word to be found only in the dictionary of fools."**
> — Napoleon Bonaparte

"Your thoughts and your attitudes play a pivotal role in your success."

— Paul J. Meyer

Chapter #3
Choose Where to Send Your Mind

— *You can decide what goes in because you do it on purpose!*

Let me ask you some questions:

- Have you ever been discouraged?

   I have.

- Have you ever been down?

   I have.

- Have you ever been depressed?

   I have.

- Have you ever been hit from every direction by hurdles, obstacles, or problems in your home or in your business?

   I have.

"Where you are and what you are will always be because of the dominating thoughts that occupy your mind."
— Isabelle Meyer

A FORTUNE TO SHARE

If you answered "yes" to one or more of these questions, I urge you to take out a piece of paper and make a list of all the negative events or circumstances you experienced in the last year. (At the very least, take a few seconds and make a mental list.)

Be sure to think of everything — every downer, everything that has turned against you in business, every problem at home — every trouble in every single area of your life. Write them all down.

Next ...

> **I would like you ...**

> **to ceremonially ...**

> **shred ...**

> **burn ...**

> **or bury ...**

> **your list!**

This is what I call putting something in your "forgettery."

A "forgettery"

A "forgettery" is an idea I have taught to small children. One day, we would make an imaginary "forgettery" box and then have everyone march up and put the list of all the bad things that had happened to them in the box.

> ## "Let nothing dim the light that shines from within."
> — Maya Angelou

Then we would use our imagination to visualize burning the whole box and its contents.

The next step is really exciting!

Make a list of everything you still have:

Two hands: I've seen people with no hands.

Two legs: I saw a man with only one leg.

Two eyes: I have a dear friend who is blind.

Two ears: My mother's hero was Helen Keller, who could neither see nor hear.

Family: I read recently of a man who lost his entire family in a fire.

Your mind: I have a neighbor who developed Alzheimer's and cannot remember much of anything.

The beautiful world around you: The sky, the sun, the moon, the rain, the flowers, the colors of butterflies, the birds singing, the grass, music, poetry, good books.

Your business: The banks are still full of money, people still have plentiful savings, and there are countless jobs available.

> **"Thoughts lead on to purposes; purposes go forth in action; actions form habits; habits decide character; and character fixes our destiny."**
> — Tyrone Edwards

Be thankful, always!

Beginning when I was little, my mother instilled in me the belief that it was right and good to always be thankful. She taught me to face each new day as a gift, a reason for celebrating.

To regain an attitude of celebration and thankfulness, consider this: if it were the first day in your new business, the first day of a new job, the first date, or the first day of a dream vacation ...

- **Would you get up a little earlier than usual?**

- **How would you dress?**

- **What would you have for breakfast?**

- **Would you let minor inconveniences get you down?**

- **How much energy would you have?**

It would be incredible! How positive and excited would you be as you entered the day, simply because you were concentrating on the positives?

When I consider these questions myself, I feel like jumping up and down with excitement. *Just thinking about the power of thoughts and attitudes energizes me.*

I know the climate I create through my thoughts and attitude is the only environment I will ever live in. For many years these affirmations have helped me create my own "ecology":

"What is your purpose? What is your attitude? When you find one, you will find the other."

— Paul J. Meyer

- When it is pouring down rain, **I choose to see the sun**.

- When it is dark at night, **I visualize the moon**.

- When there is adversity, **I develop an attitude of gratitude and list all the things I am thankful for**.

As you keep your blessings in mind, you tend to increase them. According to the law of attraction:

> *You actually bring favorable circumstances and conditions into being by thinking about and concentrating on the positives in your life.*

Marcus Aurelius long ago stated that the world we live in is created by *how we think*. If you disdain, resent, or view pessimistically your life condition, then your awareness of blessings begins to shrivel up and you believe they have become fewer in number.

The opposite attitude — *concentrating on the positive* — helps create the opposite results.

Life continues, blessings increase, well-being flourishes, and circumstances prosper above and beyond, exceeding our greatest expectations.

I have seen this in my life and the lives of many others.

Focus on the "haves," not the "have nots"

In any culture or any country, it is easy to fall into the habit of dwelling on adversities. Watching television, reading the news-

> **"Vision is the art of seeing the invisible."**
> — Jonathan Swift

paper, hearing people everywhere talk about the negatives all lead you to think of the minus factors in your own situation instead of the plus factors.

When you indulge in this negative mental thinking,
it becomes a destructive habit.

You may even reach the point where you are emotionally paralyzed, unable to handle life's daily unthreatening routine.

But you can still change!

When you concentrate on what you have *going for you*, you create a right attitude, you snap out of worry or depression, and then you go forward!

When you concentrate on the positives in your life ...

you stir up the desire to get moving,

to conquer every adversity that jeopardizes your well-being or prosperity,

to take advantage of every opportunity that comes your way,

to seize the day,

to take action, and

to create opportunities that do not yet exist.

"No matter what the statistics say, there's always a way."
— Bernard Siegel

Being thankful for what you have creates a twinkle in your eye, a spring in your step, and a magic sound in your voice. A thankful, positive attitude is dramatic, magnetic, and electrifying.

How much more productive would you be if you adopted this attitude? How much more successful would you be?

This attitude is a gift, and it is your choice whether or not you accept it. It is a gift I chose to accept from my mother. *It is one of the greatest lessons I learned from her!*

This lesson has provided me a magic carpet that has taken me everywhere in the world, and it has made available to me vast opportunities to help many others use more of their God-given potential.

Don't let yourself be limited

I went to a public school, but at the same time I feel as though I were "home schooled" because my mother made a special project of affirming — and reaffirming — the positives in life by frequently asking me:

"Did they tell you about anything in school today that you couldn't do, or that couldn't be done?"

Sometimes I would report a teacher saying something like, "You have to be in a certain place to do this or that," or "You have to have a certain education to do this or that."

"If it's true that the only limitations are the limitations we place upon ourselves, then it would certainly make sense to remove all limitations yesterday!"

— Paul J. Meyer

To these limiting comments, my mother would say:

> **"Just remember that if there's anything you want to do, the only limitations there will ever be are the ones you place in your own mind. Where you are and what you are will always be because of the dominating thoughts that occupy your mind."**

You can choose to limit yourself … **<u>or not!</u>**

"He who believes is strong; he who doubts is weak. Strong convictions precede great actions."
— J. F. Clarke

"Stay on track to achieve your success."

— Paul J. Meyer

Chapter #4
The Power of Focus

— Lessons from a magnifying glass!

Do you possess the ability to focus with the intensity, concentration, and commitment of a laser?

If not, you should!

Do you know the power of a laser?

> A laser produces a thin, intense beam of light that can burn a hole in a diamond, carry the signals of many different television pictures at the same time, drill eyes in surgical needles, remove diseased body tissue in surgery, or even monitor shifts in the earth's crust. When a laser beam is concentrated on one small area, it can produce temperatures higher than 5500° Celsius.

How do you learn to focus on a job with similar intensity?

Seeing the light

Let this story help explain how. One afternoon, my father said he wanted to show me something. He took out his magnifying glass (it was about four inches in diameter) and held it steadily about an inch away from the fender on our old car.

I was astonished at what I saw happen! The sunlight went through

---

"Obstacles are those frightful things you see when you take your eyes off your goal."
— Henry Ford

---

the magnifying glass, transforming into a burning white light. A small column of smoke appeared, and then the paint began to bubble and peel off, right before my eyes.

My father explained:

> "Just like the magnifying glass focuses the light into a powerful force, your ability to focus can help you reach your goals. **Focus the whole weight of your personality toward a job; give the job the full impact of your total attention and concentration.**"

To help make his point, my father then held my hand under the magnifying glass until I hollered, "Ouch!" The burning heat on my hand, along with my father's words, made the lesson of the magnifying glass unforgettable.

A long time after the magnifying glass lesson, lasers were developed to concentrate a beam of light. Whether a magnifying glass or a laser, the concentration of light and energy produces phenomenal results!

As I began teaching others about motivation and success, I coined the phrase **"wearing success blinders."** When people wear success blinders, it means that they:

> **look neither to the right nor left,**

> **neither up nor down,**

> **but only straight ahead.**

They develop the capacity to ignore distractions.

"Success requires the vision to see, the faith to believe, and the courage to do."
—Charlie "Tremendous" Jones

They are able to shut out the entire world of distracting sight and sound.

With total focus, they are blind and unhearing to anything but the object of their desire.

The big payoff for me came in making individual sales one-on-one.

I focused totally on the sales presentation with the full weight of my personality.

I focused my presentation in a narrow beam aimed directly at my prospect.

I captured all my energy and channeled it as a powerful force to help me communicate with my prospective clients.

What happened? *I sold a LOT!*

My prospects were always overwhelmed by the attention and focus I gave them. I was fully committed to fill whatever need they had, so far as my abilities would reach.

I was in my mid-twenties when I fully realized what an incredible asset this intensity and focus on success could be. I was in the life insurance business, selling for the nation's largest exclusive weekly premium life insurance company. This company offered a variety of policies. I felt my best bet, however, would be to study their rate book and figure out which policy would fulfill the greatest need for the greatest number of prospects I had at that particular time.

I memorized the rates and did not use the rate book. Ninety percent

---

"Your ability to focus is the most important success skill you can ever develop."
— Brian Tracy

of my sales were on one special policy. I became a specialist — an expert — with this one contract.

Because of my focus and specialization, **I led the company and broke every record previously set in that company since its founding 50 years earlier.**

Eyes on the prize

I followed the same plan when I worked for the largest exclusive ordinary life insurance company. I specialized on a specific market — airline pilots — and a specific policy. I had more success with those pilots than other insurance agents who were promoting a wider range of policies.

Again, I was the leading producer in the company. That is the way it went throughout my insurance career:

focus,

specialization, and

setting sales records!

When I trained other life insurance agents, I emphasized the importance of choosing a specific market. In training sessions, I would take out a city map and explain, "If you drive an hour to work, you are wasting precious time each day."

Then I would ask a sales rep where he lived. I would then circle an area around his home that he could reach within 15 minutes. **Then with a brush and dark ink, I would blot out the rest of the map.**

> **"It is a rough road that leads to the heights of greatness."**
> — Latin Proverb

A FORTUNE TO SHARE

This was a visual, powerful reminder of the principle of focus.

I would tell them, "Carry this in your car with you and concentrate on it. This is where you should prospect. This is where you choose to sell. This is where you build a network. This is where you earn your living."

I also told them to study the traffic patterns in their city and make sure they were never on the streets during the busiest traffic times because that was a waste of their most valuable resource — time. I emphasized, "**Focus all your time and effort in one area**."

Over the years, I have been intrigued with what the Apostle Paul wrote in a letter to some first-century Christians:

> "This one thing I do — forgetting what is behind and straining toward what is ahead, I press on toward the goal to win the prize."

I carry this with me on an affirmation card. It is deeply etched in my mind. *Focus! Press on!*

Focus maximizes success potential.

It enhances creativity.

It increases imagination.

It expands vision.

It multiplies inventive ability.

"Just don't give up trying to do what you really want to do. Where there are dreams, love and inspiration; you can't go wrong."
— Ella Fitzgerald

When I am focused on successfully achieving my goals, I can dismiss worry, fear, and indecision. I have no time to dwell on the past, no time to be discouraged by what others say, think, or do.

I direct all of my time and energy
toward my current project.

I approach everything with full effort and attention. I know no other way. People sometimes are astonished or even amused by my intensity. I can be in a conversation or conference in my office when the phone rings, but I do not hear it. Another person walks into the room, and I do not see that individual.

I am completely immersed and focused on the person and the situation before me. The ability to focus magnifies for me the urgency and excitement of the project at hand. The needed action steps emerge into camera-sharp clarity.

The opposite of focus

Think about the opposite of focus, the inability to focus on the one project you are working on at the moment.

I must ask·

- **Can you ride two horses at once?**

- **Can you swim two rivers at one time?**

- **Can you hold two thoughts in your mind simultaneously?**

> **"Focus on the right subject to get a desirable picture."**
> — Paul J. Meyer

43

- Can you participate effectively in two conversations at once?

- Can you straddle a fence indefinitely?

- Can you feel full of fear and full of faith at the same time?

- Can you get to second base with one foot planted securely on first?

- Can you fly to two different destinations at the same time?

- Can you serve two masters at one time?

The answer is obviously "no possible way" to each of these questions ... but why do so many people think they can?

They try to.

They think they can.

They hope they can.

But it's completely impossible!

The principle of focus and specialization is evident among successful people everywhere. Professional athletes specialize in one sport, doctors specialize, and lawyers specialize. A focused strategy results in sustained success and provides superior profits.

For example, in the motivation companies I have founded since

---

"People with goals succeed because they know where they're going."
— Earl Nightingale

1960, we continue to focus and concentrate on delivering the very best products, the very best training materials, and the very best service-consciousness for helping people develop their full potential.

When I started SMI, I focused on the life insurance industry because I had a strong background and knowledge of the people and needs in that industry. As a result, 90% of all the personal sales I made during the first two years were to the life insurance industry. Then it branched out from there.

Interestingly, more than 70% of our sales have been made with one program: The Dynamics of Personal Motivation. **More copies of that program have been sold than the distribution of any other self-improvement program in history.**

Focus! Focus! Focus!

What is the most important thing about taking a picture? Sure, it needs to be in focus, but the most important thing is this: your subject!

A boring but well-focused photograph is still pretty worthless!

In business, you must not only "do things right" but also "do the right thing." Like selecting the right subject for a photo, so focusing on the right work is what it takes to succeed.

My God-given potential has given me both the right and the responsibility to choose goals and set priorities in all areas of my life.

No one else knows which goals are most appropriate for me, and no one else should dictate my priorities.

"The price of greatness is responsibility."
— Winston Churchill

A FORTUNE TO SHARE

Just as my father showed me how to control the awesome power of a magnifying glass and just as scientists direct the miraculous laser beam to perform incredible feats, **I alone am personally responsible for my life and what I do with it.**

And so are you!

Like a laser or a sunbeam through a magnifying glass, I can burn with focused, amplified levels of energy. When I empower myself to focus on what means the most to me, my success surprises even me!

Let it ring true for you as well!

> **"People seldom see the halting and painful steps by which the most significant success is achieved."**
> — Anne Sullivan

"As soon as you become indispensable, you will truly be indispensable."

— Paul J. Meyer

Chapter #5
How to Get Ahead

— *Starting up the ladder of success*

A rising star in one of my companies pulled me aside one day and asked me, "How do you get ahead around here?"

This young man, by the name of Ferrell Hunter, would go on to accomplish great things in my company and in life, and I believe it was due to his desire to be more, to have more, and to get ahead.

Here is what I told him:

#1: Do more than you get paid for

I was reared to do the best I could, to believe that the primary consideration was not what I was paid. I believed my most important considerations were:

> **productivity,**

> **efficiency, and**

> **effectiveness.**

> "No one ever attains very eminent success by simply doing what is required of him; it is the amount over and above the required, that determines greatness."
> — Charles Kendall Adams

48

Early in my life I developed the keen sense of responsibility and obligation to be fruitful and profitable for my employer every hour, every day. This philosophy has served me well, and as I have observed others who got ahead in their careers, I have seen this philosophy hold true.

**The best advice is to always do more
than you get paid for.**

In contrast to doing more than you get paid for, today a culture springing from the 1950s and 1960s seems to be common. A comedian I saw at a dinner theater demonstrated this culture. The setting was a restaurant looking for some new employees. A disheveled young man responded to the advertisement.

When he came in to talk to the manager, he said, **"Hey, you the boss? Come here."**

The owner responded, **"Yes, are you looking for a job?"**

The young man said, **"I don't know. I need to ask you some questions first. How much time do we get off during the day for breaks? How much vacation time do we get? How much sick leave do we get, and what are the other benefits?"**

"Well, come in," the owner said, **"and let's talk about the job."**

The young applicant said, **"I don't want to know about the job until you answer my questions."**

Yes, the skit was exaggerated (just a bit), but it's closer to reality than any business owner would like to admit.

> **"We must always change, renew, rejuvenate ourselves; otherwise we harden."**
> — Goethe

But the truth is, employees need to know what is expected of them ... so they can exceed those expectations! I told Ferrell that doing more than you get paid for always pays off.

Some practical applications of this attitude include these:

- **Take pride in your work.**

- **Always make sure it is "better than average."**

- **Get to work early, not "just in time" — and *never* late.**

- **Stay after hours if necessary to get the job done well and on time.**

- **Identify existing problems and seek solutions — either solve the problem or offer suggested remedies to the appropriate person.**

- **Assume responsibility for your work, including your mistakes. Never place blame on others for problems.**

Doing more than you get paid for requires a fast start and keeping up that pace with the determination to do your best and reach your goals.

Ferrell took my advice and put it into action from the very beginning.

"It only takes one person to change your life – you."
— Ruth Casey

#2: Overfill your place

"Start looking around," I emphasized to Ferrell, "and find out what jobs are done within visual distance of where you are working."

- How does the shipping department operate?

- How are all the mailing lists handled?

- Who do the people in the other departments report to and why?

- How does all the equipment around here work?

I emphasized to Ferrell:

> "Trust me, if you do more than you get paid for and you start overfilling your place, management will notice that you know everybody else's job in your department. There soon will be a change in your pay, and you will be promoted. It is inevitable."

You cannot be promoted if nobody else knows your current job. The best basis for advancement is to organize yourself out of every job you are put into. *You simply cannot take this advice and not get ahead.*

I gave this same advice to our eldest daughter, Janna, when she started working at one of our companies. She began as a secretarial assistant, and then job-by-job, function-by-function, she

---

"Have a purpose in life and having it, throw into your work such strength of mind and muscle as God has given you."
— Thomas Carlyle

learned them and mastered them and was promoted to executive assistant to the president of the company. Janna became indispensable!

Overfilling your place
always pays off.

#3: Learn what the company does

Ferrell became a student of administration, supervision, and management. He took all of the courses we had and read everything else he could get his hands on. He attended seminars, conclaves, and conventions.

In addition to learning everything about our company, Ferrell also learned what the competition was doing and then offered ideas for improving our products, service, inventory control and shipping, etc.

Asking questions is a great way to learn.

And Ferrell asked lots of questions. He got to know everybody in every department and in every area of the operation. He would ask them, "Exactly what do you do in this job?" and soon became an authoritative information source.

When Ferrell first started working for our company, we had 12-inch, long-playing records with the printed scripts. (This was in the days before cassette tapes and portable recorders, and long before CDs or Mp3 players.) Even though Ferrell's job was to assemble the programs we produced, he began taking some of

---

"I am a great believer in luck. The harder I work, the more of it I seem to have."
— Ferrell Hunter

---

the programs home with him and listening to the records after hours.

Before long he had gone through a dozen of them. He knew the material well. I could see the evidence in his life. *He was becoming a product of the product.* He knew the material so well that in addition to using it in his own personal life and applying the principles within the company, he offered to teach them.

When I asked him if he wanted to do one of the training sessions at a school, he jumped at the opportunity. And at the same time, his income jumped.

Not long after, I asked Ferrell to help me conduct leadership workshops to approximately 100 audiences around the United States and overseas. He felt he was qualified and ready to assume that responsibility, and he did a great job.

Learn what your company does, because ...

When you are through learning,
you are through.

#4: Ask for more to do

Ferrell quickly gained greater self-confidence, enhanced self-image, improved managerial skills, and increased communication skills both written and speaking.

One day he surprised me when he asked, **"What else can I do?"**

> **"Try not to become a man of success but rather try to become a man of value."**
> — Albert Einstein

So we started giving Ferrell more than one job to do. He was soon involved in management, training schools, public speaking, and making some significant contributions to product development.

What happened as a result of his asking for more to do? His span of involvement in our companies broadened, *and his income went up.*

A fellow employee, obviously a little jealous of Ferrell's advancement, said to Ferrell, **"You're just lucky."**

Ferrell quickly replied, **"I am a great believer in luck. The harder I work, the more of it I seem to have."**

#5: Ask for more responsibility

Ferrell never stopped asking for more to do. At one time he was involved in helping to manage as many as 12 of our companies.

When he demonstrated capability and credibility in his current responsibility, he would ask for more responsibility in line with his interests and abilities and in line with what he thought would improve our products and service.

This is what "climbing the ladder" is all about, but each step is earned.

#6: Cross train

It has always astounded me that companies will select good people, give them responsibility and authority in a specific position,

---

"Successful people do what unsuccessful people won't."

— Byrd Baggett

---

and then almost "pigeonhole" them where they remain in that function and are never given an opportunity to learn other job functions and responsibilities in the company.

Ever heard of a "DEAD END" job?

What has made our group of companies strong is the enormous amount of cross training we have done. All of our top people could be put in almost any position in any company and operate and run it professionally.

Looking back, I realize that we changed Ferrell's title and position every 24 months ... during a period of 30 years. He has:
- packed boxes,
- supervised others who have packed boxes,
- managed a department,
- managed several companies,
- been vice president of training,
- been president of marketing companies,
- been president of manufacturing companies, and
- a whole lot more.

I have told Ferrell's story over and over to young people as an encouragement and to tell them:

> **"Life may be hard by the yard, but it's a cinch by the inch."**

Ferrell's example demonstrates that success is a journey. *You do it by climbing one step at a time and one day at a time.* It is not done overnight.

> **"Success isn't measured by the position you reach in life; it's measured by the obstacles you overcome."**
> — Booker T. Washington

A FORTUNE TO SHARE

**When it is done right and with depth,
you can do the same thing,
starting at any company, anywhere,
any time, in any position.**

If you want to open doors of opportunity, learn to ask the big question:

"How do you get ahead around here?"

**"Those who let the small things bind them
leave the great things undone behind them."**
— Scandinavian Proverb

"When you do what you love, it awakens the dream machine within!"

— Paul J. Meyer

Chapter #6
Loving What You Do

— *Work is to be enjoyed, not tolerated*

Decades ago I wrote in my journal some notes about work that later I used to write a speech called "The Joy of Work." That speech earned a first place commendation by the National Speakers Association.

My convictions about the *value of work* and my *enthusiasm for work* have been a factor in my success. I fear that work is fast becoming a lost art. Many people fail to recognize and enjoy the benefits of work:

- **Work provides an exciting, satisfying thrill.**

- **Work polishes silver and gold and refines character.**

- **Work rows life's boat upstream.**

- **Work weeds the garden and cultivates the mind.**

- **Work lifts weights and spirits.**

- **Work overcomes adversity and defeat.**

- **Work is the breath of life.**

- **Work is love in action.**

"Work is the chance to find yourself."
— Joseph Conrad

58

- Work mines coal from the earth and uncovers diamonds.

- Work supports the wings that put eagles high in the air.

- Work turns poverty into prosperity.

- Work turns dreams into reality.

The value of work

I learned early the far-reaching values and joy of work. My master teacher was my father, who came from Germany, where he worked as an apprentice for four years to become a master cabinetmaker. He made hand-carved bedroom suites that sold for five thousand dollars in the 1920s. He took great pride in his workmanship and enjoyed deep satisfaction in using skills he had worked long and hard to perfect.

Along with my father, my brother, sister, and I built our home in California. We drew the plans, mixed the cement by hand, laid the brick, threaded the pipe, installed the electrical wiring, and mixed the colors for the paint.

We did it all! The only person we hired was the man who plastered our house.

When we asked our father why we were doing all these things ourselves, he said:

"Self-discipline is actually a form of self-indulgence. Self-discipline allows you to focus on the things you want to accomplish."

— Dr. Stan Frager

"We are doing all of this so we can learn to work, to develop the habit of work, to create by our work, to enjoy work, and to feel the sense of pride that comes from work."

When we finished the job, we loved our home and were proud of it. I am thankful my parents taught me the profound exhilaration of work well done.

Short changed today

I feel sorry for many young people today who do not have the opportunities I had for work and the benefits I learned from it.

Much of what I did as a youngster would be "below" most people today. I worked in the grape vineyards with the transient workers, picked prunes and apricots, worked in a cannery, worked in a dehydrator, dug tree stumps, drove a tractor, and trimmed trees. I also had the experience of buying fruit and selling it on a roadside stand. I had the profitable experience of buying, rebuilding, and selling bicycles.

"You can do anything if you have enthusiasm. Enthusiasm is the yeast that makes your hopes rise to the stars. Enthusiasm is the spark in your eye, the swing in your gait, the grip of your hand, the irresistible surge of your will and your energy to execute your ideas. Enthusiasts are fighters, they have fortitude, they have staying qualities. Enthusiasm is at the bottom of all progress! With it, there is accomplishment. Without it, there are only alibis."

— Henry Ford

Working was a necessity back then, **and it prepared me to become an entrepreneur**.

Part of the fortune I inherited from my parents came as they taught me, at an early age, the importance of filling my life with worthwhile activities and the importance of working to *earn* what I wanted in life.

> **I learned by working that when you
> set challenging goals and discipline yourself
> to work toward them, then you can
> accomplish anything you desire!**

Work is great!

Creative expression through work

On a trip with one of my sons to South Texas to visit my brother, Carl, I enjoyed seeing my brother's face and watching his eyes sparkle as he described several of his new inventions and his futuristic plans in his field.

It was *artistry and poetry put to music*, a man in love with his work, his electric light bulb, his cotton gin, the products of his creativity, his masterpieces.

My son and I were completely mesmerized as Carl talked about the technology of a swim spa he had designed. Carl was obviously *a man in love with his work*. He was like Edison, working in his laboratory, losing all sense of time, and frequently forgetting mealtime because he loved his work so intensely.

> **"We make a living by what we get. We
> make a life by what we give."**
> — Winston Churchill

Never the same old thing

Work fills time with intensely interesting and satisfying activities. I am never bored!

I meet people all the time who are not happy in their careers, but they keep on plodding in the same old jobs, spending a lifetime *marking time, hanging on*, or *waiting for retirement*.

Why would you do such a thing!

People who do not possess a passion for their work should get out and pursue some other career. I firmly believe that people need to find work that utilizes their unique potential and inspires in them an engaging intensity.

Truer words were never spoken than those by Carlyle, the English essayist:

> **Blessed is he who has found his work; let him ask no other blessedness.**

A chance to share

Work gives people an opportunity to share something of themselves with other people. "By your fruits you shall know them" refers to spiritual things, but it applies just as truly to all realms of life.

My greatest satisfaction is pursuing work that helps improve the lives of other people. That is, "**motivating people to their full potential.**"®

> ## "When you do what you do best, you are helping others."
> — Roger Williams

62

Words from Albert Schweitzer capture my philosophy about work choices. He said:

> **"Whatever work people choose to pursue, they should make sure it is of service to other people because that provides the most long-standing satisfaction."**

I couldn't agree more!

Boost your energy

Work increases energy and the capacity to perform. If you have ever tried to jog, you find that when you first begin you are unable to run far before you feel exhausted.

If you give up at this level, you will never set any records. You can either quit, or you can keep on in spite of the fatigue.

Then you experience what is known as *"second wind."* Suddenly there is a new source, a new reservoir of strength and stamina, a new capacity for exertion.

The principle of *"second wind"* works in business just as it does in sports or any other activity.

When you get caught up in an exciting spirit of competition, you suddenly find that it is no harder to complete four or five major actions in a day than you had previously thought it was to do three.

With persistent performance at the new level, pushing against the newly attained record, you establish the new level as a habit and are ready to move to even higher accomplishments in your work.

"Within our dreams and aspirations we find our opportunities."

— Sue Atchley

Successful work increases energy
and builds greater capacity, which enables
people to perform at higher levels of
efficiency and achievement.

Work increases desire

A good friend of mine, Kurt Kaiser, a world-famous composer and pianist, gave me the best example of this principle I know. He said:

> **"The greatest composers do not just sit down and write because they are inspired, but they are inspired because they work."**

Many people have it all backwards!

They want to sit around and wait to be inspired before they do something worthwhile. *It simply does not work that way.* When people get to work on a worthwhile project, inspiration follows.

Thomas Edison said it well:

> **Success is 2% inspiration and 98% perspiration.**

Work brings rewards

Nothing is more satisfying to me than a job well done. I have never thought of work as punishment because I knew that kind of thinking would never motivate me to achieve my goals.

Working hard does have some drawbacks; it occasionally brings difficult and painful moments. There have been times when I

"Work is life, and good work is good life."
— James W. Elliott

64

wanted to chuck the whole thing. But my experience has been that for every drawback, there is a greater benefit or desirable reward.

> **One of the most outstanding rewards**
> **of work is simply the satisfaction**
> **of having completed a worthwhile goal**
> **and earning the rewards the**
> **completed goal brings.**

Tolstoy, the renowned Russian author and philosopher, offered keen insight into work when he said:

> **"The more that is given, the less the people will work for themselves."**

For me, hard work has been the way to discover the end of many rainbows.

My mother knew a great deal of poetry by heart and often quoted her favorite lines. One stanza she recounted to me countless times during my youth is now one of my favorites:

> *The heights by great men reached and kept*
> *Were not attained by sudden flight,*
> *But they, while their companions slept,*
> *We're toiling upward in the night.*

> **"The greatest composers do not just sit down and write because they are inspired, but they are inspired because they work."**
> — Kurt Kaiser

"Money is usually the common denominator in all equations."

— Paul J. Meyer

Chapter #7
Money Is Only an Idea

— Revealing the importance of money

This is not a book about money, but almost everything is really about money in some way.

**It's all about money
because you need it
to reach your dreams,
to eat, to provide shelter, and
to take care of others.**

You spend 8-10 hours a day working to get money, so it is crazy to not know more than the average person knows.

Wouldn't you agree?

Unlimited potential for growth

Soon after I turned 15, I asked my mother, "Am I going to have to do manual labor all of my life?"

The wisdom of her response profoundly influenced the direction of my life.

"It's all His by right of creation. That sums it up. That also means I know my job, title, and position: steward."

— Paul J. Meyer

She put her hands on my head — one hand on each side — and, looking me straight in the eyes, she said:

"You have everything you need right here between your ears. In your head, you have everything you will ever need to take you anywhere you want to go, to have anything you want to have, and to be anything you want to be."

I believed her. At that moment I knew the world's abundance was mine — to earn and to possess.

I could choose to remain a fruit picker, or I could stake my claim on the world's resources and riches.

The choice was mine, and everything depended on my attitude!

Over the years I have realized even more fully the powerful role attitude plays in determining success, including financial success.

- **When people think of themselves as successful, they succeed.**

- **When they think of themselves as wealthy, they usually do what it takes to become wealthy.**

In contrast, people who *feel* inferior, *act* inferior. People who consider themselves failures fail. People who think of themselves as poor remain poor. A poor self-image is an imposing, impenetrable barrier to achieving financial success.

> **"If money is all that a man makes, then he will be poor — poor in happiness, poor in all that makes life worth living."**
> — Herbert N. Casson

I have chosen to think of myself as a success!

Money ... and your attitude

Attitude toward money itself also determines financial success. What I think about the nature of money is equally as forceful as what I think about myself and my potential for making money.

And the same applies to you.

> **What you think about the nature of money**
> **is equally as forceful as what you think**
> **about yourself and your potential**
> **for making money.**

My belief that *money is only an idea*, along with my positive self-image, is responsible for my success in earning money, saving money, investing money, and in accumulating assets.

Money itself has no intrinsic value

Money is simply printed paper or minted metal worth no more than other paper or metal of comparable size and quality. **The difference is made by money's exchange value.**

Authority and power have historically been vested in ownership. The person with the most tangible goods has always had an advantage because such goods may be traded for other assets, labor, raw materials, or additional goods.

> **"In short, the way to wealth, if you desire it, is as plain as the way to market. It depends chiefly on two words, Industry and frugality; that is, waste neither time nor money, but make the best use of both."**
> — Benjamin Franklin

Since tangible wealth is cumbersome and in some cases absolutely immobile, money serves as a substitute — a token that represents valuable possessions.

The paper currency now in circulation consists merely of promissory notes guaranteed by the government. It is backed only by the faith people have in their government. The value of money lies in what others believe it is worth. Its value is based on belief and trust.

In this context, *money is only an idea*. Understanding this concept has been vitally important to my desire and ability to attain financial success.

Money is to be invested

Most people respect money. A wealthy person once said:

> **"Anyone who doesn't spend time working is a disgrace, and money that is not working is even more disgraceful; it doesn't even have any aches and pains to excuse it."**

Sharing this pragmatic attitude toward money, few wealthy people have a lot of cash because it is invested. *It is busy working for them, making more money.*

For people with wealth, money and its buying power hold no great sense of awe. It is money's investment power, *the power to multiply itself*, that commands the interest and attention of those who own it.

"A fortune is about so much more than just money."

— Paul J. Meyer

As a result, most of the world's money is invested in assets other than cash. Most business transactions go on through credit. The credit card is rapidly replacing currency for the average consumer. "Plastic money" is neither tangible nor concrete, it is merely a concept, an *idea*.

More money used than circulated

Consider this: there is never as much money in circulation as is transacted in business in a day.

For example, let's suppose I take a client to lunch and pay the restaurant $50. The restaurant owner uses the $50 to pay a supplier for fresh vegetables and other foods. The supplier, in turn, uses the $50 to pay a truck driver who delivers the food. The driver then buys food and clothing with that $50.

Transactions totaling $200 took place using only the original $50.

This illustration makes two points:

First, the importance of cash is highly exaggerated, and

Second, money is only an idea!

Money has different values

The value of money varies and depends upon what is bought, when, and where. For example, a $20 bill does not mysteriously change into a 50 or a 100, but its value varies.

"Not to know is bad; not to wish to know is worse."
— Nigerian proverb

In the hands of a foolish or extravagant spendthrift, a $20 bill might purchase only $5 worth of goods. At a different time, in the hands of a discerning person, the $20 might be used wisely to buy goods that can become worth $50.

The Bible itself says, **"wealth certainly makes itself wings"** (Proverbs 23:5).

Enjoying long-term wealth requires a watchful eye on purchases and investments *because money is only as valuable as choices make it.*

The value of money fluctuates

A familiar example of money's fluctuating value is merchants' willingness to sacrifice some profit through reduced sales prices.

This willingness to alter the value they place on their inventory is influenced by their need to secure cash, to pay taxes, to get rid of existing inventory to make room for new items, or various other reasons.

At such times, the consumers' dollar is worth more, but when shortages of some vital product cause prices to go up, the consumers' dollar purchases less.

The fluctuating value of money is only one of many variables I take into consideration when planning for my financial success. While the impulse buyer is not likely to become financially independent, I have learned by experience that *neither is the overly cautious.*

"The highest reward for a person's toil is not what they get for it, but what they become by it."
— John Ruskin

PAUL J. MEYER

**Those who genuinely know money,
with all its characteristics,
and use it with judgment and daring,
gain the prize of financial success.**

These insightful individuals literally spend their way to wealth as they wisely invest and acquire assets that appreciate in value, such as securities, real property, and equities. To those who understand money, these are just some of the ideas that money represents.

When people ask me how they, too, might enjoy the same financial success I have earned, I can almost feel my mother's hands on my head as her words echo in my memory:

> **"You have everything you need right here between your ears ... ."**

First of all, I tell them, *believe that you have unlimited potential* for financial success and growth.

Second, recognize that *you are personally responsible* for your financial achievements.

Third, develop an attitude and belief that *money is only an idea.*

"The man who will use his skill and constructive imagination to see how much he can give for a dollar, instead of how little he can give for a dollar, is bound to succeed."
— Henry Ford

73

"The key that turns risk taking into success is called *action.*"

— Paul J. Meyer

Chapter #8
Nothing Ventured, Nothing Gained

— The importance of taking risks!

You mention "taking risks" and the hair stands up on some people's necks and their breathing starts to become labored. They almost have a panic attack!

"I've been burned before," they say.

"I can't afford to fail," others say.

"My spouse won't let me," some even say.

I don't understand what all the stressing is about. *Taking risks is nothing more than taking calculated steps toward your dreams.*

Sure, you learn by experience and you get smarter, but those are by-products of taking risks. You cannot buy them in advance.

Courage to take risks

Many years ago I was in Acapulco with my friend, real estate investing expert, Mark Haroldsen. I was sitting under a palm tree at the Pierre Marquez Hotel, when Mark asked what I was doing.

"Without courage, wisdom bears no fruit."
— Baltasar Gracian

A FORTUNE TO SHARE

I told him I was writing an article, a speech, and a lesson for one of our programs, based around the *courage to succeed*.

Mark read some of my notes and laughingly said, **"Someone needs to write a book called *The Courage to Be Rich*. There is such a need for this."** I said he was welcome to borrow some of my content if he wanted to. *(He wrote the book several years later, and sold tens of thousands of copies!)*

Then Mark turned serious and said, **"Let me tell you a story."**

He went on to tell me about a seminar he was conducting for more than 1000 people. One day he asked the crowd, **"Who has been to my seminar before?"**

Most of the hands went up.

"Who has been here two times?"

Many hands went up.

"Three times?"

Still a lot of hands went up.

"Four times?"

A lot of hands went up.

"Five times?"

Mark counted, and there were over 100 people who had been to his seminars five times!

> **"All glory comes from daring to begin."**
> — Eugene F. Ware

Next, Mark asked these seasoned seminar attendees to tell about some of their real estate investments. **He discovered that very few had even made any investments!**

> **People had the information about investing**
> **in real estate, but**
> **they had not put it to use.**

It dawned on him that you can get all the information and all the education in the world, but you have to get started.

> **You have to take a chance.**

> **You have to believe in the fact that you can make the right selection, the right choice, the right decision, and you can make that first investment.**

> **You have to believe in yourself.**

> **You must *take a risk*!**

Taking risks comes down to taking action

It all comes down to taking calculated risks. You must think things through, set goals, and plan.

And then you must *take action*.

Have you ever met people who say, "I tried that once and it didn't work. So I'm not going to do that again."

"You have removed most of the roadblocks to success when you have learned the difference between movement and direction."
— Joe L. Griffith

My reply was:

> **"I once had a pair of pants that shrank, but I didn't quit wearing pants."**

In other words, it is not what happens to you, but rather it is your *attitude* **toward what happens to you**. The old saying "nothing ventured, nothing gained" is literally true.

Dangers everywhere!

Once you start focusing on risks, you will see the danger of just living!

- Getting out of bed in the morning is taking a risk.
- Driving your car is taking a risk.
- Just breathing the air might get you lung cancer.
- Going to work gives you a chance of workplace injury.
- Typing at your computer might result in carpal tunnel.
- Flying in a plane is risky.
- Walking your dog is dangerous.
- Watching TV can be bad for you.
- Eating virtually everything can cause some sort of ailment.

Stop!

People actually live very happily with real and present risks all around them … **because they have grown used to them**.

Doing anything involves some risk, from financial loss to physical harm. Successful people learn the art of "taking a calculated risk."

"To turn an obstacle to one's advantage is a great step towards victory."
— French Proverb

Learn as you go

I learn from past mistakes and previous risks. My judgment gets better, which obviously comes from experience. I make fewer "wrong decisions" each day of my life.

You cannot learn *before* you go. You must learn *AS* you go.

Today, I would say that around 90% of the businesses I start now, or invest in, succeed. In my 50s, around 75% of my ventures worked out. In my 40s, only about 50% worked. In my 20s and 30s, somewhere around 35% of my ideas worked.

I'm getting better with age, I guess! But consider this:

> In my lifetime, I have started or invested in over 100 companies. Of those, 65% did not work. But the remaining 35% succeeded! This brings my lifetime batting average to something like 35% ... and a baseball player with a .350 batting average is in the top 1% of all batters!

And one more thing: the 35 companies that did succeed, **they succeeded on a grand scale!** If it took 65 strikeouts to hit 35 home runs and a few grand slams, I'm a very happy man!

Take risks that are well thought out and calculated. Those who take foolish risks are not wise at all.

You have to step out

When I was 18 years old and in the United States paratroopers, we jumped out of planes. I knew that jumping was taking a risk, but I also knew when I was jumping, I was stretching my capabilities. I was challenging myself.

> **"Accept the risk and expect the reward."**
> — Byrd Baggett

I had zero fear.

Jumping was a well-thought-out, calculated risk. I knew what I was doing and how to do it well. It was not foolhardy.

We were told what the statistics were and what the odds were — like a million to one you were safe when you followed instructions and did what you were told.

I did my best. I knew that being a paratrooper would be a growth experience. And I lived to tell about it.

> **A life without taking risks and a life**
> **without taking chances**
> **is a stagnant and stale existence.**

To risk is to exceed your usual limits in reaching for a goal. A certain amount of uncertainty is simply part of the process.

Taking a risk is loosening up on the *known* and the *certain* and the *safe* to reach out for something you are not *entirely sure* of but that, according to your best evaluation, will work.

Risking is like jumping. Sometimes you *think* you know where you are going to land, but you are not always *certain*.

Growth requires risks

We cannot grow by staying in our comfort zone. We cannot explore our potential and expand it without taking a risk or taking

---

"Nothing can stop the man with the right mental attitude from achieving his goal; nothing on earth can help the man with the wrong mental attitude."
— Thomas Jefferson

---

a chance. Whether you are going to get closer to another person or start a business, it is all a risk.

Many people do not want to take a risk until they know that everything is exactly perfect. They sit back and wait for ...

the perfect moment,

the perfect investment,

the perfect job,

the perfect weather, or

the perfect situation.

The trouble with that approach is that it almost never comes.

Similarly, people often analyze and think about it too long. They worry. And then they simply choose to avoid all risks.

Not so with you!

Successful people take chances.

Successful people take risks.

Obviously a balance is essential between investigating and checking — studying and analyzing — and actually taking action, **but a point comes with many opportunities when you lose more by** *waiting* **and** *doing nothing* **than you could possibly gain by additional checking**.

> **"Life is either a daring adventure or nothing at all."**
> — Helen Keller

To the bold ... but not the stupid

Some people become addicted to taking scary, foolish risks because they get a euphoric "high" from the mere uncertainty of the risk.

I am not talking about these foolhardy kinds of risks at all. Everyone knows that kind of risk taking results in self-destruction. I am talking about intelligently thought-out, calculated risks.

For example, I take a risk just by driving a car, but I am very cautious. I have been driving for over 60 years and have never put a scratch on one. My father trained me to drive the most intelligent way to protect myself and those riding with me. So in that area of life I minimize the risks by being a careful, responsible driver.

I have lived a lifetime of thinking, planning, and then jumping in — taking a chance — and it has paid off handsomely for me. People ask me about different businesses I have started and how I knew when I had enough information to make an investment in real estate or any other venture.

I tell them I always ask myself some questions:

- **What are my goals?**

- **Can I reach my goal without taking a risk?**

- **What are the benefits to gain if I take this chance?**

- **What can I lose by taking a chance — by risking?**

- **What can I do to prevent these losses?**

> **"Great minds must be ready not only to take opportunities, but to make them."**
> — Colton

- Is the potential loss I am thinking about greater than the possible gains?

- Is this the right time to take this action?

- What pressures are on me to make this decision?

- What would I have to know to change my mind about taking this risk?

- What experience do I have taking this type of risk?

- Who is someone I can confide in or ask for advice about this risk?

- Do I have personal blind spots in my vision about this risk?

- If I take this chance, this risk, will people think more of me or less of me if I succeed? Do I really care?

- If a loss does occur, will I take it personally, or am I able to be realistic and objective about it?

- Will I worry and worry about the risk I have taken?

- Who else has made a similar type of investment besides me?

- What actions can I take to track my investments and protect them?

> **"Never let your fear of striking out get in your way."**
> — Babe Ruth

- How will this risk affect me, my children, my parents, my friends, my company, my relationship with any bank or institution?

- Do I really enjoy the lifestyle of an entrepreneur?

Fortunately, anything that has ever happened to me in my role as a salesperson, a businessperson, or an investor has never affected who I am as a person or reduced my self-image.

I just figure it was a risk I did not have sufficient knowledge about or that the timing was wrong. I chalk it up as experience that I could use for continuous growth as a person and as an entrepreneur.

As you take risks, make a conscious decision to maintain a healthy self-image, peace of mind, and happiness.

Own your choices

I also feel very strongly that we need to accept personal responsibility for our lives — for the choices we make and the actions we take. Being taught to take responsibility for my decisions has helped me to think more, study more, analyze more.

In addition, I rely on my spiritual beliefs to guide me and provide peace of mind about my decisions for taking certain risks. An especially powerful affirmation for me is Philippians 4:7-8:

> Be anxious for nothing, but in everything by prayer and supplication, with thanksgiving, let your requests be made known to God. And the peace of God which

---

"Remember, no one can make you feel inferior without your consent."
— Eleanor Roosevelt

---

surpasses all understanding will guard your hearts and minds through Jesus Christ.

I have to be totally honest about myself. My feelings must be unguarded at points. I must be vulnerable and open. I must exercise my freedom to be the very best person I can possibly be.

I made the decision early in life _not_ to be "a timid feeder in the lagoon." I have tried to live by the philosophy that you must take a risk if you want to sail out, head home, and fight the windswept loam with the cargoes of the world.

> **It is not the gale but the set of the sail
> that determines which way you go.
> That is the choice of the navigator.**

I have always asked myself, "Am I the navigator of my life?"

Are you the navigator of your life?

Do NOT let fear hold you back

What is the opposite of taking risks? It is suffering from the paralysis of analysis and the fear of taking a chance, the fear of getting out of a comfort zone.

When I played tennis competitively, I would go to the tennis club and there would be so many people who never did anything but hit from the ball machine, or hit on the backboard, or practice serves. I never saw them play very much. The same applies to golf. How many people just stay on the driving range!

"Effort only fully releases its reward after a person refuses to quit."

— Napoleon Hill

A FORTUNE TO SHARE

Some people earn degree after degree. The university becomes a cocoon, a womblike existence in an academic arena where they feel safe and secure. **No risk is involved, no chances are taken.**

In selling, this *paralysis* or *fear* is referred to as "call reluctance." Salespeople either quit selling, make fewer calls, or stay in the office and rationalize because they are afraid people will strike back where it hurts most:

at their desire to be loved,

accepted,

appreciated, and

wanted.

Nothing wrong with these things, but something is wrong if they hold you back from your goals and dreams!

So salespeople refuse to pick up the phone. They don't make the sales presentations. And eventually they fail because they fear taking a risk.

The real value of taking risks and moving into the unknown in any area is not how much money you are going to make or how big or how small the result.

**The most profound value lies
in the fact that this decision
is yours and that it gives your
life deeper meaning and provides
a wellspring of added strength.**

**"Our greatest glory is not in never falling,
but in rising every time we fall."**
— Confucius

Identifying promising opportunities, studying them, and making sound decisions — taking calculated risks — makes you feel more alive!

It makes you in control.

Don't let anything hold you back!

"Life will always be to a large extent what we ourselves make it."

— Samuel Smiles

"Go out and shake the money tree!"

— Paul J. Meyer

Chapter #9
Opportunity Is Knocking

— Did you just hear that knock at the door?

Over the years, I have made the majority of my income from *commissions* on sales and *royalties* received from writing courses (programs) sold around the world.

I have invested these funds in nontraditional ways, exposing a trait of mine — *entrepreneurship*.

I have a lot of fun in business.

I enjoy negotiating.

I love the thrill of the chase.

I like making a deal.

I hear opportunity knocking, *everywhere*. Others may miss it, but I hear it *loud and clear*. I'll be the one to jump up, grab the handle, and throw the door open wide!

Here are a few of the most unique deals I have made, and the principles I learned along the way. I heard the opportunity knocking, ever so faintly at the door.

"I am imagination. I can see what the eyes cannot see. I can hear what the ears cannot hear. I can feel what the heart cannot feel."
— Peter Nivio Zarlenga

A small ad = big opportunity!

One Sunday afternoon after church, I was reading the paper when I saw in the real estate section a small ad — *very small* — advertising an apartment complex in a city about 100 miles away. I could not imagine an ad that small for such a large apartment complex.

PRINCIPLE: Keep your eyes open, at ALL times!

Out of curiosity I called the number. An 85-year-old man answered the phone and told me he was selling the complex for a friend who was not well.

PRINCIPLE: Someone's misfortune may be your gain!

I told him I was coming down in a private plane and arranged for him to meet me at the airport. *I did not want him at his house answering the phone when others called about the ad.* I wanted to be the first one to see the complex.

PRINCIPLE: First come is often first served!

My instinct was correct! The complex was a good one at a good price. After I looked at it and we had negotiated over a cup of coffee, I asked him if he was authorized to make a deal. He said he was.

PRINCIPLE: Be curious. Check things out. Trust your instincts!

Since neither one of us had a contract form, we took the paper

---

**"Opportunities? They are all around us ...
there is power lying latent everywhere
waiting for the observant eye to discover it."**
— Orison Sweet Marden

---

place mat from the restaurant, turned it over, and wrote a contract on the back of it. I gave him $500 as a deposit with the agreement we would have my lawyer and his lawyer draw up a contract the next day.

PRINCIPLE: Act now! Be decisive!

While we were writing the contract the following day, I found out that if the owner sold the property, he would have an enormous capital gains tax. I called him and asked, "What will you do with the money?"

He answered, "Pay the tax and put the balance in the bank and live on it."

Next, I asked him what his estate would do with the money when he died. The man's wife almost started to cry and explained, "I don't know why God put us here with no children to leave it to."

PRINCIPLE: Keep the big picture in mind — the person is always more important than the deal!

I told them maybe God did give it to them so they could leave it to some children. They looked at me with a strange look on their faces.

I asked their religious denomination. They said they were Southern Baptists. "Perfect," I replied, "Why don't you give the complex to the Baptist Foundation of Texas for their Seminary?"

More strange glances.

"Nothing happens by itself ... it all will come your way, once you understand that you have to make it come your way, by your own exertions."
— Ben Stein

Then I explained, "That money could be used to train many young people to be ministers, teachers, and other Christian workers. The Baptist Foundation of Texas would take care of you the rest of your life. You could live wherever you wanted to live, drive whatever kind of car you wanted to drive, do whatever you wanted to, in exchange for the apartment complex."

> **PRINCIPLE: Think outside the box. Be creative. When it comes to money, people usually limit their thinking!**

They took my advice and donated the complex to the Baptist Foundation of Texas.

This also meant I couldn't buy it, and *I was fine with that*. It was a better deal for them, and I was glad I could help them.

> **PRINCIPLE: It's only a great deal if it's a win-win for everyone!**

A peculiar twist was that the owners were not going to give the eighty-five-year-old man a commission because the complex was a gift. At the last second, I told them I would kill the deal for them unless the elderly man received his $25,000. He received that amount. It was a godsend for him because of his age. We were close friends until he died.

> **PRINCIPLE: Stand up for others if you can!**

Interestingly, a few months later the Seminary sold me the apartment complex. I kept it for some time, filled it with tenants, and made many upgrades and improvements. **Within 12 months I sold the property and made $600,000 profit.**

"Small opportunities are often the beginning of great enterprises."
— Demosthenes

All this from answering a *one-half inch ad*!

A stunning farm in bankruptcy

A quite unusual real estate transaction began when I received a call from an attorney friend in Dallas who told me about a farm near Belton, Texas that was being sold because the owner was declaring bankruptcy. A group of real estate agents would be meeting down there for a mini-auction with plans to buy it and split it up into pieces.

The next day I went to the farm. It was in the late fall of 1986 and there was a light drizzle. The farm was completely trashed out.

PRINCIPLE: Let your mind see what could be, not what is!

It certainly did not look like it was worth what they were asking except that the site, Summers Mill, was a famous landmark, and the river was magnificent. *I had to use my imagination to visualize what could be done with the rest of the farm.*

When I asked the owner what he would like to do, he said that he would like to stay there on the farm.

PRINCIPLE: Ask what people want. It shows that you really care about them!

Next, I asked what would happen to him if the real estate agents bought it later that day. He answered that he would have to move.

> **"Half of the world is on the wrong scent in the pursuit of happiness. They think it consists of having and getting, and in being served by others. But, it consists of giving and serving others."**
> — Henry Drummond

When I told him I would buy it right now and allow him to stay, *he agreed to sell it to me!*

PRINCIPLE: If you want it, do it. Don't wait!

We wrote the agreement on the back of a three-by-five card. I gave him $500 cash as a down payment and bought it. He stayed for a year. It was a win-win situation!

The real estate agents were none too pleased! They asked the farmer why he sold it to me. He replied, "Because I trust him … and because he's the only one who asked what I wanted."

PRINCIPLE: Honesty and integrity shine through when you are real, honest, and kind!

I used the farm to raise ostriches for several years, then converted it into a retreat and conference center. Now, picturesque Summers Mill has thousands of people come through its doors every month. It is a wonderful place for businesses, ministries, schools, and others to host retreats and conferences, away from the hustle and bustle of busy city life.

PRINCIPLE: Swap horses before the one you are on falls down dead!

It's been an incredible investment, one that will continue for generations to come.

Over a game of tennis

Many years ago, I was taking a tennis lesson at the Lakeway World of Tennis from the #1 player in the world in my age group.

> **"A wise man will make more opportunities than he finds."**
> — Sir Francis Bacon

During the lesson, I noticed a lot of condominiums nearby. I asked how many there were. My instructor said there were about 100 of them altogether.

The tennis instructor explained they had not been selling well and that about 20 of them were still empty. When I asked how long they had been empty, he answered, "Two years, but you don't want to buy them. The market is suppressed and they aren't selling very well."

PRINCIPLE: Ask a lot of questions. Be inquisitive!

I found out who owned them and as soon as the lesson was over, I called. I said I would buy all 20 of them if he would finance them.

PRINCIPLE: Create win-win deals!

Crazy or not, he said he would be glad to finance them, and we closed the deal in about 30 days. I started renting the condominiums and putting them up for sale. Because I was playing a lot of tennis back then, I spent a couple days there about every two weeks.

As a result, I began to sell the condominiums, one at a time, to people on vacation I met there. I would walk around the tennis courts and say to people, "I remember when I was doing what you are doing and wished I owned one of these condominiums you are renting now."

I told them I would show them how they could own one. Over five years of going down there, playing tennis, and meeting people, I made more than $1 million profit on those condos!

"Opportunity rarely knocks on your door. Knock rather on opportunity's door if you wish to enter."
— B.C. Forbes

PRINCIPLE: Remain committed to your investment!

Even more important than the money was the fun and relaxation my family enjoyed there. It was one of the favorite places for our family to go for vacation. In addition, I sold condos to several friends who still enjoy them.

Listen for the knock at the door!

When I was a young salesman, I happened to be in a country store one hot August day drinking a RC Cola and eating a fried pie. The store was quite small — only three or four tables — and I overheard a conversation at another table. Two men were talking about some nearby land for sale that could be bought simply by paying the overdue taxes. I listened carefully, got into my Commodore Hudson automobile, drove into town, and asked where I could get some more information about this land.

PRINCIPLE: Do your homework!

As a result, I bought three lots. Next, I enlisted a friend to join me in the venture to make a profit on these lots.

PRINCIPLE: Include others if you need their help and expertise!

He built three small homes on them, each around 800 square feet, with cement floors, cement block walls, pine cabinets, and no paint. We quickly sold these homes for $4,500 and made $1,500 profit on each one. *That was quite a bit of money at that time!*

PRINCIPLE: Decide what you want to do with an investment, then do it and get out.

"We must either find a way or make one."
— Hannibal

In about 1952 or 1953, I was in a restaurant on the top floor of the Columbus Hotel on Biscayne Boulevard in Miami. I was having lunch with a man and trying to sell him a life insurance policy. I overheard J. Paul Riddle, the founder of the forerunner to American Airlines, pleading with Arthur Vining Davis to help his company, a cargo airline that was in serious financial trouble. More than 80 years of age at that time, Davis was the retired chairman of the board and cofounder of the Aluminum Company of America.

PRINCIPLE: Learn about the decision-makers in your area or industry!

Davis finally consented to lend Riddle several million dollars. When they reached across the table and shook hands, J. Paul Riddle said, "You are an angel."

PRINCIPLE: Don't talk confidential business in a restaurant or public place.

I told my prospect I had to go to the restroom because I was not feeling well and took the elevator down 12 floors to the Francis DuPont securities firm on the ground floor. I went in and told the broker I wanted to buy 100,000 shares of Riddle Airlines at $0.40 a share.

PRINCIPLE: Be bold!

He asked if I had ever bought stocks before, and I said, "No."

He asked me if I knew that the company was in trouble, and I said, "No."

PRINCIPLE: Don't take "no" for an answer!

> **"There is one thing stronger than all the armies in the world, and that is an idea whose time has come."**
> — Victor Hugo

I bought the stock for $40,000 dollars — *money that I did not have* — rushed back upstairs, and completed my insurance sale. After lunch, I called my friend Bill Armor and we went to several banks. Finally, one of Bill's friends loaned me the money largely on the basis of his respect for Bill and their friendship.

In a little over six months, *the stock went up to over $5 per share!*

My $40,000 investment had grown to $500,000, so I decided to sell, but the broker told me that if I dumped that much stock on the market all at once, the stock would drop to $2 per share.

So I went to the Arthur Vining Davis estate, sat by the gate, and waited until he came home in his limousine. His security guards stopped me, but Davis asked what I wanted. I told him I had some stock that no one would buy. He took me into his den and I told him exactly how I got it.

> **PRINCIPLE: Speak up. Go to the top, if need be, and tell them your story. Do what it takes to get the job done.**

He said, "**That's a great story, young man. You will do well in life.**" He bought the stock from me, and I made almost $500,000 as a result.

Turning curiosity into millions!

Several years ago, I was walking along a pristine beach on a Caribbean island when I noticed a completely trashed out piece

> **"It's choice, not chance, that determines destiny."**
> — Conway Stone

98

of property, sandwiched between a nice hotel and lovely condo-
minium.

It was dark, empty, and obviously hadn't been lived in for many
years. Out of curiosity, I jumped the fence.

PRINCIPLE: Be curious! See and hear what others miss!

I looked around the property. The house was small, the grounds
were in horrible condition, but the beach was stunning, the view
was incredible, and the location couldn't have been better.

It was then that I saw a very old For Sale sign, laying flat on the
ground. I brushed off the leaves and dirt and called the number
on the sign.

An old man answered the phone. I told him where I was and he
said, "Oh, that property has been in litigation for the past 10
years."

**PRINCIPLE: Don't let someone's negativity dampen
your creativity!**

I asked, "Can you check to see if the lien has been lifted?"

He agreed to, and hung up. A few minutes, he called me back.
The property was cleared the week before! But then he added,
"Before you think of buying it, the fellow who owns it lives in an-
other country, and he's a crook."

PRINCIPLE: Keep knocking!

> **"There will come a time when big
> opportunities will be presented to you, and
> you've got to be in a position to take
> advantage of them."**
> — Sam Walton

The old man was still an active real estate agent, so I asked him to start the contract process. My contract and my offer, with the help of my attorney, was sufficient to get the property.

Interestingly, before the contract was signed by the owner, I was offered my asking price, PLUS an additional $2,000,000 for the property!

> **PRINCIPLE: Once you find something special, others will come and want to buy it from you!**

I chose to hang on to the property, enjoyed the property for several years, and then sold it for many times more than what I had paid for it. *It was one of the best real estate deals I have ever made*, and I would have completely missed it had I not been curious enough to jump the fence and call the number on the For Sale sign.

In that instance, the sound of opportunity knocking on the door was very, very faint.

> **PRINCIPLE: Be alert. Be observant. Keep your ear to the ground!**

Opportunity is everywhere!

I can hear it. Can you? *Opportunity is knocking at your door right now!*

Opportunities come in different forms, so be ready. Perhaps it will be:

> **"To remain as you are denies who you can be. Life is what you make of it and achieving full potential is an everyday choice."**
> — Larry Jones

- an idea in your head

- a need left unmet

- a hunch in your gut

- an old For Sale sign

- a question left unanswered

- a deal a friend doesn't want to pursue

- an ad in the paper

- words from a song

- an image on TV

PRINCIPLE: Create your own luck!

Opportunities are everywhere, in every town, with every person you meet, in every book you read, and everywhere you drive your car.

Are you looking for a great opportunity?

You should be.

Are you expecting a great opportunity?

You are now!

"When fate hands us a lemon, let's try to make lemonade."
— Dale Carnegie

"To excel, ignore your weaknesses ... and focus on your strengths."

— Paul J. Meyer

Chapter #10
Maximizing Your Strengths

— This is where you can really soar!

Pete Fountain has enjoyed renown and notoriety as a world-famous clarinet player. Not only have I enjoyed listening to him play the clarinet, but I also like him as a person. I got to know him when I bought his 1936 four-door convertible.

Several years ago, our World Convention was held in New Orleans, Fountain's hometown. Coincidentally, our convention theme that year focused on maximizing strengths, and Fountain just happens to be one of the most impressive examples of maximizing strengths I have ever known.

When Pete Fountain was still a young teenager, he began to play the clarinet. Almost immediately he knew he had found his strength.

His teachers, however, told him not to bring his clarinet to school. They said he needed to join an athletic team and have fun like other boys. But he refused to listen. **He knew he was not a boy who played the clarinet** — he was a *clarinet player!*

Fountain invested all his energy in his music and became the number one jazz clarinetist of his time. Pete Fountain *maximized his strengths*!

"Continuous effort, not strength or intelligence, is the key to unlocking our potential."
— Liane Cordes

Putting your mind to it is NOT enough

A popular myth says we can do anything if we put our mind to it. That sounds inspiring and a bit noble, but it simply is not true.

Physical limitations, for example, keep many people from doing some things they might like to do. I know some very short, thin people who like football, but it is obvious that no matter what they do, they can never play on a professional football team.

Take me, for another example. I love football, but considering my age, height, and weight, you can imagine what would happen if I were hit by a lineman on any of today's teams. I would be carried out on a stretcher!

In our self-improvement business, we teach people about the amazing power of desire and motivation. But we *also teach them* to be realistic and discerning about our different gifts and strengths.

When people ask me what accounts for my success in life, *I point out how I have concentrated on my strengths instead of my weaknesses* — my potential, propensities, and possibilities instead of perplexities and problems. I bask in the sunshine in my life as much as I possibly can, rather than hiding from the dark, the clouds, and the rain.

Special wisdom may be required to discern the personality traits that enable us to do one thing or prevent us from doing something else. An abundant amount of desire and motivation can compensate for certain personality tendencies, *but I have noticed over my lifetime there are some firmly established*

> **"Ability is what you are capable of doing. Motivation determines what you do. Attitude determines how well you do it."**
> — Lou Holtz

personality traits that simply will never change.

For example, I am not the personality type who would enjoy preparing accounting reports. If I had to spend most of my day analyzing figures and producing reports, I would soon cease to function effectively.

I avoid tasks that use my weaknesses. Instead, I hire people who have skills I do not have and I delegate the work to them. This keeps me free to exuberantly pursue opportunities and responsibilities that *maximize my strengths*.

A legacy of strength

I am the beneficiary of an incredible heritage. *My mother and father gave me a fortune when they conditioned me in a positive, creative way.*

I started my first self-improvement company because I realized that the majority of people were not as lucky as me.

Most people have been:

- *victims* of negative conditioning

- *programmed* to fall short of using their potential

- *conditioned* to fail

The only way these countless individuals could reprogram themselves was to throw their conditioning out the window and concentrate on their strengths instead of their weaknesses.

"The heart of a fool is in his mouth, but the mouth of a wise man is in his heart."
— Benjamin Franklin

Thoreau, an early American essayist best known for his attacks on the ineffective practices of social institutions, insisted that people must use their strengths even when they are different from the strengths of most other people. He said individuals often called nonconformists are those who possess the invincible courage to "march to a different drummer."

The emasculating philosophy dictating that you should follow a certain pattern uses these words:

"would"

"should"

"must"

"ought"

"do it my way"

"my way is the only way"

Many parents, for example, are obsessed with the idea that their children must go to a particular college, perhaps because they went to that college or because that college is prestigious. I am convinced that some students would be better off attending a two-year college or a technical school. In addition, some parents almost insist on their children's pursuing a certain career, without study and analysis of their children's strengths.

People have frequently asked me how I have known what my strengths are. I tell them it is a process of self-evaluation.

"Success seems to be largely a matter of hanging on after all others have let go."
— William Feather

Ask yourself:

- **Am I using my strengths?**

- **When am I most creative?**

- **Do I have the ability to form relationships with other people?**

- **What gives me the greatest sense of fulfillment and happiness?**

- **What is my personality type?**

I feel even more strongly today than ever that the quest for identifying, evaluating, and using my strengths has been well worth the effort.

Does It move you?

One of the foremost indications I am using an inner strength is experiencing a *sense of excitement* about developing and using it.

Even if putting the strength to use requires work, it is not drudgery. I have fun using it! I love to write, for example, and enjoy each stage of developing a new program. The sense of excitement I experience is obvious evidence that when I am writing, I am operating out of an inner strength.

Another example relates to salespeople. Many individuals in sales have told me they enjoy a feeling of exuberance when making a sales presentation to a client.

> **"Let me tell you the secret that has led me to my goal — my strength lies solely in my tenacity."**
> — Louis Pasteur

But people who do not like sales will fear it, can never get it right, are sapped and drained at the end of the day, and are probably operating out of a weakness. A career in sales is not an intelligent choice for those people, and they should consider pursuing some other career.

Does it make you better?

Another benchmark I have used to determine my strengths is the magnitude of my motivation to use and develop those strengths and abilities. Even though they may have been undeveloped at the time, my way of thinking about them convinced me they offered possibility and I was eager to work on them.

I knew early in my life that my strengths were in the areas of people skills, persuasive skills, selling, and entrepreneurial activities like starting businesses. That was what I liked to think about and where my motivation and desire increased as I developed these skills.

In contrast, one of the greatest horrors of my life occurred when my father took me to a foundry to explore the possibility of working there and pursuing a career. I had never been in a foundry where they make patterns and cast objects in metal. It was dark, smelly, and noisy, and I felt absolutely zero interest in it.

My instinct, my gut reaction, everything within my inner being knew, "This is not a place for Paul J. Meyer. This is not where I want to be!" I also knew it was a place where Paul J. Meyer was never going to be.

Do you pick it up quickly?

Another evidence of using one of my strengths was how quickly

---

"When you cease to dream you cease to live."
— Malcolm S. Forbes

---

and easily I learned a skill or activity. When I improved steadily with anticipation of getting better quickly, I was confident I was operating out of an inner strength.

When I consistently performed with excellence over a period of time, I also knew I was operating out of one of my strengths. I knew, for instance, when I started selling, it was an almost in-born strength. I love to sell. It is a joy for me. It is simple. It is easy. I am highly productive, effective, and efficient when I am selling. Over time, I have not grown tired or bored with selling. Selling is obviously one of my strengths.

Does your self-image improve?

Another clear indication I am operating out of an inner strength is feeling positive and confident and having a good self-image when engaging in an activity requiring that strength.

I guard against over generalizing because I recognize that when we begin a new skill, we do not usually feel 100% positive about it. If we are operating out of an inner strength, however, after a small amount of experimentation and trial and error, we can sense fairly accurately whether this is something we are going to feel good about doing.

People with low self-esteem imagine they have only weaknesses. So they fail to recognize their strengths but spend their time worrying about improving their weaknesses. They could improve their effectiveness and their self-image if they would put their weaknesses on the back burner and concentrate on their strengths.

Because this strategy enhances a positive self-image and max-

> ## "Luck is what happens when preparation meets opportunity."
> — Elmer Letterman

imizes productivity, I have persistently applied it in my own life.

When I am operating out of one of my strengths, the activity regenerates me and creates additional energy. Practicing this strength motivates me and reinforces an already positive self-image.

The benefits of strengthening your strengths

Some years ago, a reporter asked the coach of a Chinese Ping-Pong team how the team practiced. The coach said they spent at least eight hours every day practicing their strengths. This type of practice developed strengths to the maximum and strengths compensated for their weaknesses.

He gave a further example of one of the players hitting every ball with a forehand. The player did not have a good backhand, so he just used his forehand so efficiently he could not be beaten.

This simple illustration is a great reminder to apply the same principle of maximizing strengths in every area of life.

"I am *stressed out* if not *burned out*," a business associate told me several years ago.

"I am glad you have admitted your plight to me," I told the associate. I continued, "I often wondered why you had chosen that line of work. I think it is simply not based on your strengths as I have observed them."

This man immediately pursued other career opportunities and is now happily working in a job that minimizes his weaknesses but

---

> **"Think like a man of action and act like a man of thought."**
> — Henri Bergson

---

maximizes his strengths. I see absolutely no evidence of his former complaints of being stressed out or burned out.

Know when to move on

How does this apply to me? When I grow disinterested in certain entrepreneurial pursuits, I simply change directions to something that does engage me, motivate me, and bring out the best in me.

Or I delegate. Delegating has been one of the greatest boons to my being able to maximize my strengths. I delegate responsibilities or tasks I am not particularly good at or do not have any interest in.

An example in my personal life is handiwork around the house—that is one area I simply do not like. I do not want to use my energy on doing something that takes away from tasks and responsibilities I am genuinely interested in and good at.

Or paperwork. I do not like to do it, so I delegate most of it. Delegating frees me to pursue activities that I enjoy and that have a high payoff.

Review your success list

The crucible test of using my strengths is reviewing my successes. Keeping a list of my successes and reviewing it tells me at a glance what works best for me.

When I hit tough times — as all people do from time to time —

> **"Know the value of time; snatch, seize, and enjoy every moment of it. No idleness, no delay, no procrastination; never put off till tomorrow what you can do today."**
> — Earl of Chesterfield

A FORTUNE TO SHARE

I do not dwell on the weaknesses or the bad times. Instead, *I do a mental 180-degree turn to remember past successes and past pleasures.* Reliving the thrill of my accomplishments reminds me to rivet my attention on what I do best so I can maximize my strengths.

"The mass of men lead lives of quiet desperation," observed Thoreau. Decades ago, when I first read his writings, I made a conscious decision and a conscious commitment never to fall under the umbrella of that observation.

I have kept this commitment!

How?

By minimizing my weaknesses and maximizing my strengths.

"Above all, challenge yourself. You may well surprise yourself at what strengths you have, what you can accomplish."
— Cecile M. Springer

"Your job is to get over, under, around, or through every obstacle in your way!"

— Paul J. Meyer

Chapter #11
Why Negative Capability Is Your Friend

— This is the secret to turning lemons into lemonade!

I was over 50 years old before I heard the term *"negative capability."* I possessed the quality personally but had never identified it by that label.

A fabulously successful Singapore businessman, Y.Y. Wong, is the first person I ever heard applying this term to the business world.

Mr. Wong, a billionaire, operates a group of companies all over Asia whose products are concentrated in several areas, including business machines, computer systems, consumer electronics, telecommunications, financial services, and more. Mr. Wong told me that in the context of business, *negative capability is the ability to bounce back from failure by overcoming obstacles.*

Mr. Wong also said that **he had learned everything he knew about** *success* **from his** *failures.* He did this by analyzing why he failed and then by turning the negatives of failure into positives for success. He wasted no time in worry, doubt, or frustration over why he was facing obstacles.

I found as we talked that Mr. Wong's experience had closely paralleled my own.

> **"Progress always involves risk; you can't steal second base and keep your foot on first."**
> — Frederick Wilcox

For him and for me, achieving success has been influenced largely by the ability to *ignore the negative forces* in the environment and to refuse to allow them to control today's and tomorrow's actions.

The English poet John Keats originated the term "**negative capability**" and defined it as:

> **the condition in which "individuals are capable of being in uncertainties, mysteries, doubts, without any *irritable* reaching after fact and reason."**

Examples are everywhere of people who have used negative capability:

- Everyone knows **Barbara Walters'** name and face from TV, but a lot of people may never know that she lisped when she first began her career. As a result of much work and effort, she overcame and has since made her mark as an outstanding broadcast journalist.

- Though a quadriplegic confined to a wheelchair after a tragic diving accident, **Joni Eareckson Tada** paints, writes, and travels the world over, challenging people to consider their positives or strengths and not their weaknesses.

- I was always impressed by **Jim Abbott**, the famous baseball pitcher who was born without a right hand. He would rest his glove on the nub of his right hand, deliver a pitch — at 90 miles per hour — and quickly switch the glove to his left hand. With only one hand, Abbott does not think of himself as disabled. He concentrates on what he can do, not on what he cannot do.

I have held fast to the attitude that *failure is final only* if I quit

---

"There is no education like adversity."
— Benjamin Disraeli

---

trying. Giving up after a mistake or failure steals the opportunity for success in the future. Instead of despairing, I ask myself these questions:

Why did I fail?

What can I learn from this experience?

How can I avoid making the same mistake again?

With this approach, mistakes and failure can be transformed into stepping stones to success.

Prepare to win

No matter how strong my positive mental attitude might be and no matter how carefully I choose friends and associates from positive, enthusiastic people, I am realistic and realize there will come times when I must deal with negative people.

For example, when I was released from military service and felt ready to make my mark in life, I decided I wanted to sell insurance. After a number of rejections, I was finally hired by one company and told to ride with several other salespeople to a sales meeting. In the car I listened and tried to learn all I could from what the experienced people said.

Imagine my surprise when we reached our destination only to be told that I was fired. "You're too shy and not outgoing enough to sell insurance" was the reason given. I wanted to say that I was listening so I could learn, but the boss would not listen.

> **"Every situation, properly perceived, becomes an opportunity."**
> — Helen Schucman

Fortunately, I did not believe his estimate of what I was capable of doing.

The road to victory was not smooth. One month I made 100 presentations without a single sale! A critic told me I evidently was not cut out to sell insurance. But I replied, "I'm going to make it next month."

And I did!

The next month was the best I had ever had, and the best the company had ever had. It happened because I refused to be "irritable" about the obstacles I faced.

Negative capability has enabled me to face unanticipated obstacles, to hear discouraging opinions and advice, and to meet failure — and still stay on track to achieve my goal.

The quality of **negative capability** is most effective when I have a clearly developed set of goals and a written plan of action for achieving those goals. A carefully prepared plan of action has provided a firm foundation for dealing with whatever might happen.

Negative capability helps me deal with adversity above the level of emotional reaction:

- **Instead of acting with irritability, I demonstrate** *calmness.*

- **Instead of exploding with frustration, I am filled with** *exhilaration.*

> **"Success seems to be connected with action. Successful people keep moving. They make mistakes, but they don't quit."**
> — Conrad Hilton

- Instead of suffering as a victim, I conquer adversity with *abundant energy*.

- Instead of wasting time and effort wondering why I face an obstacle, I *proceed* to do what needs to be done next.

You are free to take risks

Another important aspect of **negative capability** — *an absolute necessity for success* — is the freedom to take calculated risks.

Not every venture succeeds. Not every goal is easily reached. In fact, if no plan ever fails, that would be a sure sign that I am so conservative that I have not stretched to reach a new plateau of success.

In one sense, all of life is based on taking risks. Taking a risk can be reckless and foolhardy. I never take that kind of risk. Instead, my risk taking is the result of a carefully planned strategy with a sound basis for expecting success.

Several years ago I spoke to a group of college students who were part of an entrepreneurship program at their university. **They wanted to know what the important characteristics were of success for someone who wanted to be an independent business owner.**

I told them that one of the *most important traits* they could develop was *the ability to take calculated risks* and *to learn from the failures* that would obviously result from some of those risks.

> "Prepare: the time to win your battle is before it starts."
> — Frederick W. Lewis

I made a list of all the ventures I had entered that failed *(I do not like to use the word "failure" as I am never a failure, but I will use it here to define a business venture that did not work out.).* I was surprised myself to find that I have been involved in more businesses that proved to be "failures" than in those that have succeeded.

But I learned from each failure! Instead of complaining about the unfairness of circumstances or sinking into despair, I studied my actions to discover what had gone wrong. Then I incorporated the principles I learned from studying the failure into my planned actions for later ventures.

Negative capability enables me to assume a genuine sense of positive expectancy. When I remain calm and in control in the midst of negative circumstances, it is possible for me to believe in a bright future — to expect success in reaching challenging goals.

Negative capability and positive expectancy make it possible to dream ever larger dreams, to attempt greater projects, and to enjoy enhanced success.

Negative capability reinforces my long-standing belief that in every adversity is the seed of equivalent — *or greater* — benefit if you:

> **believe it,**

> **look for it, and**

> **work for it.**

> **"The real winners in life are the people who look at every situation with an expectation that they can make it work or make it better."**
> — Barbara Pletcher

119

"You can't do much about natural talent, but you can do everything about gaining knowledge!"

— Paul J. Meyer

Chapter #12
Knowledge Is Power

— How to use this power to your benefit

"Knowledge is power," said Francis Bacon in the late 1500s. I have always believed that knowledge is essential for success regardless of the nature of your career — CEO, manager, entrepreneur, or any other pursuit.

As a teenager, my dad advised me, *"Never take a position without first being an apprentice."*

Start at the bottom to learn and gain desire

What was he really saying? As I gained experience and business expertise, I comprehended more fully the wisdom of my father's advice. I've learned that the *most effective individuals know their business inside and outside*, from bottom to top. Many of them started out as apprentices — *learning the entire workings of their industry.*

What's more, the more I know about a business opportunity, the stronger my desire grows and the more motivated I am to work toward the achievement of my goals for this particular opportunity.

The reverse is also true. If I acquire more knowledge about an opportunity, and my desire and motivation do not also increase,

> **"It's good to master the hammer until you start thinking of everything as a nail."**
> — Abraham Maslow

121

then the particular opportunity is probably not right for me. Perhaps it would not maximize my strengths or does not appeal to my interests. In this way, *knowledge provides a crucible test for desire*. Gaining knowledge gives me a firm basis for making a decision about whether or not I want to pursue a certain opportunity.

Even if I am still quite interested in an opportunity, if I do not increase my knowledge substantially, my desire is simply not sustained. In other words:

> **a small amount of knowledge will not sustain desire or motivation.**

Once I have decided (based on the basis of a certain amount of knowledge) that I want to continue pursuing a possibility, then acquiring more knowledge always fans the flame of my desire.

Self-confidence will push you through

No doubt about it — knowledge also increases my confidence! I know from experience that my knowledge bolsters my confidence.

When I know what I am talking about, I can pursue my goal enthusiastically *because self-confidence gives me a clear vision* of my goal and *creates desire* that is strong enough to sweep away almost any obstacles.

Knowledge is more than just the acquisition of facts. It is a source of an inner quality of assurance that ignorance simply cannot match. Knowledge is the *mental backbone* that holds firm while ignorance is flabby and uncertain.

"If people knew how hard I worked to get my mastery, it wouldn't seem so wonderful after all."
— Michelangelo

Knowledge has many benefits

My oldest son, Jim, is a good example. For decades, I saw him read, study, go to seminars, and network with other outstanding attorneys. When he became a district judge, I knew why: *knowledge is power!*

In addition, knowledge helps you move faster. Jim sees many cases, as does every judge, but he knows that the time when he'll have the most knowledge about a case is right then and there. Instead of making his rulings days or months later, Jim does his best to bring closure to each case ... *when the amount of knowledge is at its highest.* This enables him to have an incredibly short unfinished case list, which is the envy of other judges.

Knowledge offers another benefit:

> **it has helped me make fewer mistakes than most other people.**

For instance, I have pursued with vengeance information about capitalism, entrepreneurship, and related topics. In addition, I also studied the opposite philosophies and concepts — communism and socialism. I looked for strengths and weaknesses of each of them, analyzing what each can do and cannot do. I am convinced that my extensive knowledge has kept any mistakes I might make to a minimum.

The formula for success

How do you get a grip on all of the information or knowledge you need to successfully pursue all your interests? I believe in this success formula:

> **"If you don't know where you are going, how can you expect to get there?"**
> — Basil S. Walsh

POSITIVE ATTITUDE
+
KNOWLEDGE
+
WORK
=
SUCCESS

Here is how I break down the process:

Step #1 — Identify common knowledge

Before I invest in any business, I *read everything* I can get my hands on about it. I *ask the experts* questions. I *listen* a lot! I make it a point to *know all* the ins and outs of the business and certainly more than the competitors know.

Step #2 — Acquire new knowledge

After learning the basic knowledge that everyone else knows about a company, industry, product, or service, I search diligently for new knowledge.

Knowledge is everywhere in this information era with the Internet, CD-ROMs, seminars and workshops, books and manuals, business publications, newsletters, the business sections of large reputable newspapers, and the list goes on and on.

I read somewhere that people have to earn the equivalent of a college degree every seven years just to keep up with all of the technological changes. I believe this is true.

> **"The person who goes farthest is generally the one who is willing to do and dare, the 'sure-thing' boat never gets far from shore."**
> — Dale Carnegie

Furthermore, I also believe there is no excuse for failing to acquire new knowledge when so many opportunities for acquiring new knowledge exist.

Step #3 — Create new knowledge

After studying information from all the various sources, then I:

think about it,

analyze it,

extract the best concepts from it,

combine the best ideas, and

create a new slant or innovative ways to provide improved products and services.

My ability to analyze information and *relate the normally unrelated* has served me well. Years ago, for instance, when I saw that my employees simply were not comprehending information I was giving them, much less using it, I began summarizing the salient points and recording them on the reel-to-reel recorders.

At the time this was a novel approach; *no one else was doing it,* and it proved fantastically effective. Later I purchased a small portable player from England. I adapted the player for use in the car so that busy people, whose time was at a premium, could listen to the tapes while driving.

> **"Don't be afraid to fail. Learn from your failures and go on to the next challenge. It's OK. If you're not failing, you're not growing."**
> — H. Stanley Judd

I have been told I was the *first person ever to do this* and that I am the father of this industry. I simply *saw a need and figured out an innovative, highly effective way to meet it.*

Step #4 — Lead and manage people who work with knowledge

I consistently share knowledge with the people in all of my corporations. I have given away enough books to fill the Library of Congress! I consistently make it a practice to encourage people to learn, to share, and to explore possible ways to do their jobs better.

My experience has proven over and over again that people, when encouraged to do so, come up with rich new ideas for improving effectiveness and productivity.

Solomon, considered to be the wisest man of all time, recorded in Proverbs 10:14, *"Wise men store up knowledge."* Solomon's statement was sound and solid then, and it is a basic success principle for us today. It has been true in my own life, and I have observed it in the lives of many others:

> **when the dynamic essentials of positive attitude and knowledge are combined, they energize actions and propel to the greatest heights of achievement.**

Indeed, knowledge is **POWER!**

"If a man empties his purse into his head, no man can take it away from him. An investment in knowledge always pays the best interest."
— Benjamin Franklin

"When it comes right down to it, success is a choice."

— Paul J. Meyer

Chapter 13

Choose to Succeed

— *Success is, after all, your choice!*

If success were an accident, then none of us would have much control over our lives, our attitudes, and our destinies. But the good news is, **we do have control**.

Success is a choice.

Sure, unexplained things can happen, but I firmly believe that "**luck**" is where preparation and opportunity meet. You have to do your part.

It begins with these 10 core beliefs about success.

10 core beliefs about success

1. Winners are **not** born … they are made.

2. The dominant force in your existence is the way you **think**.

3. You can **create** your own reality.

4. There is some benefit to be had from **every** adversity.

> **"There can be no failure for a man who has not lost his courage."**
> — Orison Sweet Marden

---

5. Each one of your beliefs is a **choice**.

6. You are **never defeated** until you accept defeat as a reality and stop trying.

7. The only real limitations on what you can accomplish are those that you *impose on yourself.*

8. You already possess the ability to **excel** in at least one key area of your life.

9. There can be no great successes without **great commitment**.

10. You need the support and cooperation of other people to achieve any worthwhile goal.

Choose to have focus

Focus stimulates your desire to be a winner. This principle can be understood with these two facts:

1. **It's an attitude before it becomes an action!**

2. **It's a journey more than a destination.**

The characteristics of desire are best visualized in the word **D-E-S-I-R-E** itself. Each letter tells us how to "stand firm" on our first sure step for developing the power of Focus. Notice that these are all *mental* (improving **focus**) before they are *physical*.

"It sometimes seems that intense desire creates not only its own opportunities, but its own talents."

— Eric Hoffer

D: **Decide** … Winners make the decision to "pay the price!"

E: **Enthusiasm** … Winners have controlled, up-beat, exciting DESIRE!

S: **Synergy** … Winners know that they "multiply" together!

I: **Improve**…Winners inspect and improve their personal efforts!

R: **Remember**…Winners remember their personal goals of commitment!

E: **Energy**…Winners know that mental toughness produces physical energy!

Focus Demands Your Discipline to be a Winner. Discipline begins with a definite decision by you. You must take it personally. That is because the principle of discipline is always proactive:

- **Discipline always <u>increases</u> concentration.**

- **Discipline always <u>focuses</u> on winning goals.**

- **Discipline always <u>builds</u> confidence.**

- **Discipline always <u>produces</u> winners.**

- **Discipline always <u>improves</u> performance.**

"Get the facts first. You can distort them later."

— Mark Twain

- Discipline always <u>creates</u> rewards.

Focus strengthens your determination to be a winner

Determination is a "must" step, a "natural" step and an "automatic" step for a winner. **BUT:**

- You have to **believe** to become determined!

- You have to **consciously decide** to become determined!

- You have to **act on** your decision and belief!

Determination is built on **confidence** — you will be confident in your **identity, abilities, and strengths.** Determination is also built on **emotion** — you have extra effort every day.

> **You start emotionally focused and continue emotionally strong.**

> **You save emotion energy for creative and productive work.**

> **You don't waste emotion energy when you're focused!**

Choose to avoid negativity in your life

Negativity is the major stumbling block when it comes to **change**.

> **"You have to have confidence in your ability and then be tough enough to follow through."**
> — Rosalyn Carter

The following are some tips to help assess the negative influences in your life:

1. **Reassess all your long-standing beliefs.**

2. **Monitor your self-talk for one full day.**

3. **Examine negativity.**

4. **Make a list of all your assets and liabilities.**

5. **Accept that some failure is a part of the achievement process.**

6. **Re-program your subconscious.**

7. **Set positive-belief goals.**

8. **Associate only with positive-belief winners.**

Choose to keep your word

An employee once came into my office and confided in me, "I don't think I have much longer to live. Would you please make sure my wife is taken care of?"

I was caught completely by surprise. Nothing was wrong with him physically, but for some reason he didn't think he would live much longer. My immediate response was, "Let's get a life-insurance policy on you."

Now it was his turn to think I was joking, but he went ahead and

---

"For the resolute and determined there is time and opportunity."
— Ralph Waldo Emerson

---

got a policy, naturally passing the physical exam since he was in good health. *Less than 90 days later he was dead from a brain aneurysm!*

Though the company had taken out the life-insurance policy, I had made his wife the beneficiary. In addition to that, I paid her half of her husband's regular salary for 17 years until she was able to get her Social Security funds. I also had someone manage her insurance money so that it would keep growing and so that she could live in the same house, drive the same type of car, etc.

Why all the effort and expense, even though I wasn't legally bound to lift a finger? Because I chose a long time ago to be a man of my word, regardless of what it might cost me, because *my word is my bond.*

Get it in ink!

Since the 1950s, things have progressively changed:

from a handshake,

to a signed piece of paper,

to a 10-page document,

to reams and reams of paper.

Contracts are not what they used to be!

Every year, people become less and less trusting and more and

---

"Six essential qualities that are the key to success: sincerity, personal integrity, humility, courtesy, wisdom, charity."
— William Menninger

---

more suspicious. The increase in the size of contracts — and in the number of lawyers required to explain them — *is further indication of the increased lack of trust*. Whether it is from greed, dishonesty, mistrust, or as a result of being abused and mistreated, it is sad to see the way the world has changed.

I was not raised that way.

Over and over it was pounded into my head to be honest, which always included being:

1. **Dependable**

2. **Accountable**

3. **Reliable**

4. **Credible**

I was taught that you should say what you mean and mean what you say; and that whether you said it or put it in writing, you could be trusted to do what you agreed to do. As a result of being honest, I believe God has honored me, protected me, and blessed me.

The value of keeping your word

People believe and trust me because I keep my word. They do so not because I say I will do a certain thing, *but because I actually follow through and do what I say I will do.* Intuitively it does not seem that difficult to keep your word, but the increasing number of broken promises proves otherwise.

> **"To endure is greater than to dare ... to keep heart when all have lost it — who can say this is not greatness?"**
> — William Makepeace Thackeray

Businessman Bill Nix stated that trust is:

"The foundation on which our relationships are built. Promise keeping is the adhesive, the substance of our character that prevents the foundation of trust from cracking."

He also pointed out that discrimination lawsuits in the workplace have increased by 2,200 percent since 1980!

This is the result, I believe, of promises not being kept. *If people forget a promise they made, I do not believe they are in any way excused from keeping their word.*

Either they should learn not to make a promise they won't keep, or they should write it down and store it for safekeeping. The fact is people don't usually break just one promise — **they break many promises**.

I take what I say so seriously that I update my will regularly, writing into it the promises that I have made to certain people and marking off the promises that I have fulfilled.

I reason that if I can't do what I say I will do, then I have no right to even open my mouth to speak with other people. Not only is my word my bond, but it is a measurement of me as an individual.

What's more, I recognize that to accomplish anything in life, I need other people. If I break my promises, there is no possible way I will reach my goals — *it just won't happen*. People are

---

"Who steals my purse steals trash ... But he that filches from me my good name, robs me of that which not enriches him, and makes me poor indeed."
— Shakespeare's Othello

---

vital to every goal and keeping my word to them is of paramount importance.

People don't trust you

People are not as trusting these days, but can you blame them? Do we, and society as a whole, act in a trustworthy manner? We should, but it seems that a few bad apples always spoil the bunch.

During a two-week trip several years ago, a friend of mine and I happened to meet seven different young people who all dreamed of going to college. I met them beside the road, in restaurants, etc. I asked them questions and told each one that I would help them go to college and that they ought to write me a letter in 30 days telling me what they planned to do with their degrees.

Believe it or not, only one of them wrote me! This young lady got her wish — I put her through college — but I never understood why the other six individuals never took me up on my offer.

Perhaps they had been burned too many times in the past to believe that I was for real. Maybe they forgot. Or maybe they thought I was a little crazy. I don't know, but they lost out.

I believe we should do what we say. Our "yes" should mean "yes" and our "no" should mean "no," just like Jesus stated in Matthew 5:37.

Trust, respect, increased business, growth, peace of mind, and much more would come as a result. *Imagine what the world would be like if we all kept our word!*

"Keep your promises, even if others fail in keeping the promises they make to you."
— Bill Nix

The mutual benefit of keeping your word

I believe completely that keeping your word is just as beneficial to others as it is to you. A long-time friend of mine, the late Larry Burkett, once had a brilliant, highly efficient secretary working for him.

When the accounting department needed additional help, Larry transferred her to that department, thinking that she would be a tremendous asset there as well. However, she performed miserably.

Every few minutes she would get a drink, talk to someone, and then slowly return to her desk. Instead of firing her for doing such a poor job, Larry probed a little deeper and found that she hated numbers but loved people. Wisely, he quickly put her back at the front desk and she blossomed again.

Not long after, another businessman offered her a similar front-desk job that would triple her salary. Larry recommended that she accept the offer, and then recommended to her new boss that he always keep her in her area of gifting — to his and her mutual benefit.

That is what keeping your word is all about, and what's more, the benefits often continue for months, years, and even decades!

Keeping my word — for good

When people promise me something, I believe they will do what they say and make a note to remind them in a couple weeks of their promise.

> "They're only truly great who are truly good."
> — George Chapman

At that point if they say they are not going to follow through on what they promised, I erase from my mind the promise they made.

Though disappointed, the fulfilling of the promise rests in their hands, so I release them from it and do not hold it against them. Doing this constantly encourages me to be a man of my word.

There was a time in my life when it seemed like everyone and everything was against me. The insurance company I worked for went from boom to bust in one weekend when the owners simply walked away, taking every dollar and piece of equipment with them.

I could have walked away as well, and was even advised to do so by lawyers, **but I chose to stay behind and help put the pieces back together**.

When it was all over, I had used over a million of my own hard-earned dollars to fix what I had not broken. At that precise moment I realized that all the money in the world could never be more valuable than my word — *because my word is my bond.*

Choose to have determination

Determination gives you **perspective**:

- You focus on your strengths.

- You see the "total picture."

- You sense clients' actions and reactions.

> **"I do the very best I know how—the very best I can; and I mean to keep on doing so until the end."**
> — Abraham Lincoln

- You refuse to be distracted.

Determination gives you **persistence**:

- You will not quit on any sales presentation.

- You will not step down or stay down.

- You will not give in!

Determination gives you **patience**:

- You keep your goal in mind.

- You keep your commitment to self and team.

- You keep the pressure on yourself.

- You keep coming back…every day!

Determination gives you **power**:

- You recognize your synergy strength and your clients' need.

- You react with positive emotion.

Choose where you want to go

I was **not** voted "most likely to succeed" when I was in high school. Perhaps you were, but most of us were not.

What does that mean? *Absolutely nothing!*

"Desire creates the power."
— Raymond Holliwell

A FORTUNE TO SHARE

Your attitude is 99% of any equation. Whatever it is that you are pursuing, know that with the right attitude, you have most of the problem already figured out!

Take my word for it.

Now, your attitude is your choice. Seek to fill your thoughts, heart, and mind with the truth. **That truth might not be your current reality, but it shows where you are going.**

Choose where you want to go.

"There is always room at the top."
— Daniel Webster

"You will win if you will always get up one more time."

— Paul J. Meyer

Chapter 14

The School of Hard Knocks

— The best schooling in the entire world!

I did go through the school of hard knocks. I lived in a different era. But it doesn't matter how smart you are or when you were born or where you live, *you are going to get knocked down*.

Get ready for it.

Don't get mad when it happens.

And if you can't adjust, you'll miss it.

But if you *can learn*, if you can find the good in what you find in front of you, and if you can keep your direction clear, **it's just a matter of time before you break free and reach your dreams!**

Learning the hard way

Thousands of people over the years have asked me, "Where did you go to school?"

I simply tell them, "**The School of Hard Knocks**."

I also tell them I love the school I attended because the campus has no boundaries. It is out on the highways and byways of America

---

"There are no secrets to success. It is the result of preparation, hard work, learning from failure."
— Colin L. Powell

---

and all around the world. It is in the cities, and it is in the rural areas.

This school **requires NO**:

pre-registration,

deposit,

qualifying exam, and

entrance interview.

This school is available to anyone who wants to attend, is willing to actively participate, and is serious about learning lessons for living.

I am especially grateful for all the students I have met in my many classes at the School of Hard Knocks. The students come from everywhere. They also come in every size, shape, and age you can imagine. They are both male and female. This special school maximized the advantages of diversity long before anyone ever heard of quotas or affirmative action.

The breadth of courses and the depth of the subject matter are incredibly impressive. More classes are offered than in Harvard, Yale, Oxford, the Sorbonne, the University of Tokyo, or other great institutions of higher learning.

In the School of Hard Knocks, you learn the subject, not how to take a test. Learning is long-term, not short-term.

"Remember you will not always win. Some days, the most resourceful individual will taste defeat. But there is always tomorrow."
— Maxwell Maltz

Another feature I like about the School of Hard Knocks is that *the best students never graduate!* The most effective learners continue their education at this alma mater for a lifetime.

"**Black and blue**" are the well-earned colors of my school. They come from the bruises and hard knocks that diligent students receive from participating in the rigorous curricula.

My children and grandchildren are curious about our school motto: "**One more time!**" That is how many times I will get up after someone knocks me down, criticizes, or attacks me. Refusing to stay down, I get up and enter the game of life even more enthusiastically than before.

There are *no short courses*, *no quick fixes*, and *no free lunches*. The professors do not hand out education in tablet form for students to swallow quickly and be on their way along the road to success. And they do not give education in pre-chewed and predigested pabulum. I learned to bite off a lot, and I learned to chew a lot. I had to work to absorb it and to apply it.

In the School of Hard Knocks, I have learned some incredible attitudes and principles for success that have served me well for a lifetime.

Seize the day!

Those courses teaching this success principle have been the most fun! I have loved learning to develop a seize-the-day attitude — staying alert, being a good listener, having my radar out for every opportunity to meet people and to expand my horizons.

I have spent many hours of trial and error learning in the laboratory

> **"All things are difficult before they are easy."**
> — John Norley

PAUL J. MEYER

of life to turn theory into practice — to dream new dreams and set higher goals.

The words of William Shakespeare remind me of the importance of a seize-the-day attitude:

> **"There is a tide in the affairs of men, which, taken at the flood, leads on to fortune; omitted, all the voyage of their life is bound in shallows and miseries."**

I have learned to seize the day by seeing the potential in other people and encouraging them to use it, having a loving heart and a forgiving spirit, and helping as many people as I can in as many ways as I can and in as many places as I can for as long as I can.

Take personal responsibility

What I have learned about responsibility in the School of Hard Knocks has not been confined to the classroom; *it applies to every area, attitude, and action of my life.*

It is one of the most useful courses — one I recommend for everyone. When you accept personal responsibility for your life, the whole world looks different. When you know it is up to you, you prepare better, study more, learn more, and have greater resolve.

When you accept personal responsibility for your life, you also learn to use more of your God-given talents.

People who accept personal responsibility take more initiative and show more self-reliance. **Since there are fewer and fewer people who are willing to take personal responsibility, you stand out.** When you learn to accept personal responsibility, you

---

"Self-motivation is the 'turbocharger' of life."
— Byrd Baggett

145

are recognized as a leader and more opportunities for advancement come your way.

Schools of higher learning require studying the classics. One nugget of wisdom I remember from Plato summarizes responsibility:

> **"Take charge of your life. With it, you can do what you will."**

Think outside the box

Learning to set my imagination free, to be creative, inventive, and resourceful, and to think beyond the obvious was another exciting course that has served me well.

Teachers always have a list of terms for their students to memorize, and I remember an excellent definition of creativity:

> *"Creativity is looking at what everyone else looks at but seeing what no one else sees."*

Being creative involves these capabilities and attitudes:

- **Relating the normally unrelated.**

- **Seeing potential and possibilities others never see.**

- **Seeing stepping stones where others see stumbling blocks.**

- **Seeing possibilities where others see problems.**

"Let common sense and common honesty have fair play, and they will soon set things to rights."
— Thomas Jefferson

- Seeing solutions where others are blinded by insurmountable circumstances.

These nontraditional, innovative ways of looking at the world have helped me create the ideas for each and every business I have started over the past 60 years.

The idea for my brother's first fiberglass business came from relating the normally unrelated. My idea to start Success Motivation Institute in 1960 and put condensed information on LPs came from seeing potential and possibilities that others did not see.

The money I have made in real estate has come from seeing what other people could not. I learned early in my life that real intelligence is the creative use of knowledge — *not merely the accumulation of facts*.

Thinking outside the box was fairly easy to me as an adult because my parents taught me the basics when I was young. For instance, once when I was with my dad shopping in San Jose, California, we went into a model shop where model airplanes were sold.

I wanted to buy a model airplane, but my dad said, "No. Design your own."

I did not know anything about building model airplanes. After a "healthy discussion" with my father, he agreed to let me buy one airplane so I could learn how to build one. The next one I had to design and build myself, using only raw materials. (You should have seen the planes I made!)

Using my mind to think outside the box helped me become more

> "Failures are divided into two classes —
> those who thought and never did and those
> who did and never thought."
> — John Charles Salak

imaginative, inventive, and creative than my counterparts and has been both personally satisfying and professionally profitable.

Never, never, never give up!

I have learned through this school that in every arena — every phone call I make, every letter I write, every business deal I consider — *never to give mental recognition to the possibility of defeat.*

This approach provides me with an invincible attitude that *I can and I will.*

If life is easy for a person, with few or no changes or challenges, that person must be coasting downhill, taking the course of least resistance. Although this was *one of the most difficult principles to learn*, I saw others demonstrate again and again that the downhill road requires minimum effort and leads nowhere special.

People have to work and push to make anything go uphill. The trail to the mountain top, the pathway to the stars, demands **work** and **persistence**.

I have learned that 90% of all failure comes from quitting too soon, so hanging on with persistence has given me the best possible chance of reaching my goals. Nothing in the world can take the place of determination. Talent will not, genius will not, education will not. *Hanging on until success comes is the essence of determination and persistence.*

My all-time favorite quote about determination and persistence

---

"The difference between greatness and mediocrity is often how an individual views a mistake."

— Nelson Boswell

---

comes from Winston Churchill. He spoke these memorable words at a crucial turning point of World War II:

"Never give in, never give in, never, never, never, never — in nothing, great or small, large or petty, never give in except to convictions of honor and good sense."

Honesty pays off

"Honesty is the best policy" was instilled in me as a way of life by my parents. If any prerequisite was required to succeed in the School of Hard Knocks, this was it. I learned early that life is made up of our choices.

The doors we decide to open or close each day direct our lives and determine our destiny!

The impact of even the smallest decisions we make is captured by these lines:

Sow a thought, reap a habit.
Sow a habit, reap a character.
Sow a character, reap a destiny.

Using honesty and integrity as my basis for every decision has also helped me guard against the fatal habit of not making decisions when they need to be made.

If people will not decide, then in effect they have already decided because, as William James, the great psychologist, put it:

> **"Life is no brief candle to me. It is a sort of splendid torch which I have got hold of for a moment, and I want to make it burn as brightly as possible before handing it on to future generations."**
> — George Bernard Shaw

"When you have to make a choice and don't make it, that in and of itself is a choice."

I read an article in the *Wall Street Journal* pointing out what I learned long ago in the School of Hard Knocks. The article reported that a consultant firm asked numerous top executives to cite the primary factor in their success. *Integrity* was consistently given as one of the top five reasons for personal and business success.

My father and mother would both be proud that I have earned a good grade in this course.

Live life passionately

Learning to live life fully and savoring each moment of it is one of the most satisfying aspects of the School of Hard Knocks. Theodore Roosevelt, the 26th president of the United States and a Nobel Peace Prize winner, offered a challenge I have incorporated into my own philosophy of living life passionately:

> *"Far better is it to dare mighty things, to win glorious triumphs, even though checkered by failure, than to take rank with those poor spirits who neither enjoy much nor suffer much, because they live in the gray twilight that knows neither victory nor defeat."*

I have learned to live my own song because when I am singing my own song it comes from my heart. I have studied the lyrics, the harmony, and the melody. *I simply do not see how people*

"In all giving, give thought. With thoughtful giving, even small sums may accomplish great purposes."
— Fred G. Meyer

---

can sing a song they have not lived.

People without passion, with no zeal for living, are only a dormant force, only a possibility, like an immobile stone waiting for the blow of the iron to give forth sparks.

Living life passionately requires continuing education based on the premise that nothing grows unless it is green, and anything that is fully grown is ripe and will soon rot.

Living life passionately fuels:

> **the fire,**

> > **the desire,**

> > > **the dynamic motivation behind every worthwhile purpose, and**

> > > > **the joyous pursuit of simply being alive.**

In the graduate course of living life passionately, I learned to avoid worrying. Instead, I climb more mountains, walk on more beaches, watch more sunsets, cry when something touches my heart, and laugh when something tickles my funny bone.

My affirmation for living life passionately is Psalm 118:24:

> **"This is the day the Lord hath made; I will rejoice and be glad in it."**

"The moment you let avoiding failure become your motivator, you're down the path of inactivity."
— Roberto Goizueta

Live with a servant's heart

In the School of Hard Knocks people are given awards, trophies, and other types of recognition for outstanding contributions of one kind or another.

The most prestigious awards, I have observed, go to those who render service to others. *That is the way it should be.* As for me, I do not measure success by how high I climb but by how many people I bring with me.

I measure my success by how well I motivate people to use their full potential.

The top professors in the School of Hard Knocks seem to agree that the greatest leaders are those who serve others:

- Ghandi said, **"You will find yourself by losing yourself in service to other people, your country, and your God."**

- Socrates said, **"All people have one goal — success or happiness. The only way to achieve true success or happiness is to give yourself completely in service."**

- Albert Schweitzer said, **"I do not know what your destiny will be, but one thing I know, the only ones among you who will be really happy are those who will have sought and found how to serve."**

- The Scriptures say that **the one who will be greatest among you will be servant of all.**

"Yesterday is a canceled check; tomorrow is a promissory note; today is the only cash you have—so spend it wisely."
— Kay Lyons

The final exam

When I started out as a serious student in the School of Hard Knocks, I was mostly raw material. But as I worked my way through the courses, every knock enhanced my understanding and helped me grow wiser, and every knock opened a door to a greater possibility.

By applying the principles learned in the School of Hard Knocks, I have been honored with five honorary Doctorate degrees. What you gain in this school is noticed by others ... *and it's worth every ounce of sweat and blood!*

I have learned first-hand the truth in the Russian proverb that says:

> **"The same hammer that shatters the glass forges the steel."**

I have also learned to appreciate more fully the striking symbolism in the fact that a diamond and a chunk of coal are, in the beginning, the same. *The difference is in the final result.* The diamond has gone to the School of Hard Knocks; it has been subjected to long and intense pressure to make it indestructible, beautiful, and more valuable than a chunk of coal.

After many decades in the School of Hard Knocks, hopefully a little bit of diamond is beginning to glimmer through. I feel somewhat more like a diamond, *but I know I will need polishing for the rest of my life*.

"It is only because of problems that we grow mentally and spiritually. It is through the pain of confronting and resolving problems that we learn."

— M. Scott Peck

"Give more than you received. That is where things get exciting!"

— Paul J. Meyer

Epilogue
It's Your Fortune to Share

— you have it in you!

The stories I have shared in this book illustrate *what* I have learned and *how* I have learned it. I have earnestly tried to live out what I have learned.

Incorporating the lessons of life into my everyday attitudes and actions *has been the key to whatever success I have achieved.*

I am thankful to my parents for the magnificent fortune I have inherited by having their genes, living in their home, and being exposed to their thinking, teaching, training, and attitude.

It is my intention to pass this inheritance on as best I can to my children, to their children, to my friends, to my colleagues, to my clients, and to everyone who crosses my path for as long as I live.

You have a fortune to share, just like I do. *It is your attitude,* just like it is my attitude. *And it's your choice,* just like it's my choice.

Let's share our fortune freely.

> **"The greatest discovery of any generation is that a human being can alter his life by altering his attitude."**
> — William James